AlphaPussy

AlphaPussy

How I Survived the Valley and Learned to Love My Boobs

by GINA GERSHON

BROOKLYN, NEW YORK
Publishing books since 1997

All rights reserved. No part of this book may be reproduced, stored in a retrieval system, or transmitted in any form, by any means, including mechanical, electronic, photocopying, recording, or otherwise, without the prior written consent of the publisher. Some names in this volume have been changed by the author in order to avoid money-grubbing lawsuits.

Published by Akashic Books
©2026 Gina Gershon

ISBN: 978-1-63614-281-4
Library of Congress Control Number: 2025940993
First printing

EU Authorized Representative details:
Easy Access System Europe
Mustamäe tee 50, 10621 Tallinn, Estonia
gpsr.request@easproject.com

Akashic Books
Brooklyn, New York
Instagram, X, Facebook: AkashicBooks
www.akashicbooks.com
info@akashicbooks.com

For Mignonette Von Koppel

Table of Contents

Preface: Boobs Changed My Life 9

Part I: The Valley
    The Setup 17
    Danger in the Trees 19
    Little Miss Funtime 27
    Busted 30
    The Bully 37
    Pinball and Porn 41
    Ain't the Marrying Kind 47
    The Fort and the Football Player 52
    Sleepovers 55
    To Thine Own Clit Be True 59
    The McMansion 66
    Thrifty Balls 71
    Baseball and Boobs 76
    One of Our Cheerleaders Is Missing 81
    Vampire King 86

Part II: Schooling
    Playboy Mansion 93
    Hustling 102

The Magic People *114*
College Daze *121*
Fuck-You Money *130*
Chippendales *139*
Direct Yourself *147*

Part III: Reel Life
Auditioning *153*
My First B Movie *158*
Back in the Apple Again *162*
Sibling Rivalry *170*
Players *175*
Emotional Detachment *185*
"I Think I'll Call You Ghee-na" *190*
This Will Destroy Your Career *197*
Snatches of *Showgirls* *203*
Know Your Line *214*
Doggy Chow *219*
The Seven-Thousand-Dollar G-String *221*
Bedazzled Bondage *227*
Out-Crazy the Crazy *232*
Who's the Lezzie Now? *239*
Driven *247*
Rock and Roll Saved My Life *251*

Afterword: President of the Girls League 261

Preface
Boobs Changed My Life

Being a tomboy in my youth, I was always playing sports with the guys—baseball, football, dodgeball, you name it. But when my little buds started to blossom, I was terrified that my relationship with the bros would change.

How right I was.

I grew up in the San Fernando Valley in the 1970s—right smack in the middle of the explosion of porn. Our local family theater turned into a triple-X adult movie house around the same time my blossoms turned into bona fide boobs. This book tells stories of how I survived the Valley with a C cup, and how I later survived Hollywood, autonomy intact.

I've certainly had an unusual career. It hasn't been very commercial, and it's hardly been conventional, but I've been fortunate enough to experiment and play with different art forms—acting, singing, touring with a band, writing, directing, and producing. In doing so, I've had to constantly fight for what I was passionate about. There were parts that I had to leave my agents over because they thought they would "ruin my career," roles I had to turn down because I thought they would sully my soul, and humans I had to navigate and deter in order to protect myself both mentally and physically.

Maybe I'm a jack-of-all-trades and a master of none (although I would argue that I'm a damn fine Jew's harp player). I may not have an Oscar, but how many actors can say they've played Carnegie Hall (three times so far, but who's counting)? I'm super grateful for my wild and unconventional life.

I now find myself being the older person on the set telling stories and cautionary tales to my fellow actresses. As I've shared my experiences—navigating shark-infested waters as a teenage girl in the Valley, avoiding dangerous situations as a student living in New York City, beginning my professional career as an actress, dodging sleazy bullets in Hollywood—I've started to see a through line, a constant maneuvering and manipulating that has stitched together the seemingly random stories of my career.

These tales are about more than just being an actress—they're about being a female in the world, and about how I became an AlphaPussy in order to forge my life and career in a world full of bullies, predators, and assholes.

Anyone who knows anything about raising male kittens knows that you need to show them who's boss early on or else suffer the consequences. For instance, if you're having a staring contest with your furry little friend and you lose, rest assured, he will attack you.

He will mercilessly jump on your head, savagely bite your face, and gnaw on your hair. If you allow this to happen, he will then dominate as the alpha male and you will become his little bitch. He will wake you up and make you feed him whenever he feels the urge. Four a.m.? Why not? He will either start making strange noises, incessantly jump back and forth over your head, knock your favorite crystals off the table, or perhaps stick his cute little paw in your sleeping mouth until you succumb to his entitled needs.

This is why I strongly encourage anyone with a little tomcat to dominate them right off the bat. Unless, of course, you enjoy being a subordinate underling, powerless and weak, victimized by this cute monster. No? I didn't think so. Please allow me to share with you what I have done for years that has proven effective:

When engaged in the aforementioned staring contest, DO NOT AVERT YOUR EYES, even for a moment. He will look at you. You will stare back. You mustn't blink. Ground yourself. Steady your breathing. You need to be, or at least appear to be, confident and calm. After around twenty or thirty seconds, a minute at most, he will yelp a tiny sound of defeat as he breaks eye contact and either move away or, even better, roll on his back in submission, recognizing you as the AlphaPussy.

I've learned over the years that this technique is also highly effective when dealing with aggressive *humans* as well—men in particular.

※ ※ ※

I was so excited when I'd finally landed the part of Cristal Connors in *Showgirls*. I'd had other supporting roles in films by that stage, but this was the first lead in a big movie with an A-list writer and director. Paul Verhoeven and Joe Eszterhas were hot, coming off their enormous success with *Basic Instinct*, and were known for strong female characters. Months earlier, in Manifesting 101 mode, I had written down exactly the type of role I was yearning to play: *a strong, smart, sexy, dangerous woman, who has a sense of humor . . . and it would be great if I could dance in the part.* And get this—I added that I'd like to be in a film with the same sort of impact that *Basic Instinct* had had on Sharon Stone, who would end up becoming my cousin-in-law. So random. More on that later.

It's a wonderful feeling when people ask what I'm doing—especially in Hollywood, where I always somehow feel like a schmuck—and I can proudly talk about the project I'm working on (assuming I'm working on a project I am indeed proud of). I've now had a long, strange career as a working actor and have been fortunate to collaborate with some wonderful people, but at that point my experiences had mostly been humbling.

I imagined how great it would feel when asked the ever-present question, "What are you working on?" I would casually reply, "Oh, I'm starring in the new Verhoeven/Eszterhas film, *Showgirls*." The recipient of this fantastic news would fawn all over me, kissing my ass as they suddenly remembered a project they had that I would be absolutely perfect for and could they send it to my agent and please could we have a lunch?

The responses I actually got, however, turned out to be quite a bit different.

I remember the first time some guy—some studio executive type, smarmy, self-satisfied, confident that his position was an aphrodisiac to any starlet or struggling screenwriter—asked me what I was up to. When I told him, his eyes shamelessly dropped down to my chest and blatantly stared to the point that I felt the need to cross my arms, take a few steps back, and opine about Paul Verhoeven's Dutch films: "He's such a visceral filmmaker. His use of camera movements that mirror the emotionality of the scene is thrilling! Without any dialogue, one senses the raw truth of a situation, *blah blah blah* . . ." I babbled awkwardly, trying to talk my way into the respect I so clearly wanted.

And yet, this kept happening. By the fifth time some professional dude gave me a sleazy once-over after hearing I was going to be in this much-anticipated film, I had a flash, and recalled my basic cat training.

I stared at that male beast without blinking and said, "Oh yeah, it's going to be great. I kiss guys. I fuck girls. I dance naked. I can't wait." I knew not to break eye contact, or else pay the consequences. After a beat, the animal averted his eyes and backed away—making me the winner in the game of dominance. *Who's the AlphaPussy now, motherfucker?*

Instead of having power over me, this worm became my inferior. It was fun to see this slick, cocky facade of a man be reduced to a humble, stuttering, obedient boy. Many men will try to dominate you if you let them. Especially the insecure ones. The bullies. The ones who are still fighting unconscious battles with their disapproving daddies or overcontrolling mommies. The ones whose own dark shadows take over when they can't seem to get what they want.

PART I
The Valley

I wanted you.
And I was looking for you.
But I couldn't find you.
I wanted you.
And I was looking for you all day.
But I couldn't find you.
I couldn't find you.
—Laurie Anderson, "Walking & Falling"

The Setup

My mother was six months pregnant before Dr. Lazarus informed her that she was going to have a baby. Not only was she sick with the mumps, often missing her period, but she was, in fact, using a diaphragm—so the news of her pregnancy was quite a shock. To me, not so much. I'd been there for a while now. Just becoming.

An ear on Monday.

Tuesday, a few organs.

A few weeks later, ta-da: a foot!

I wasn't that impressed with myself, it's just what I did. No kvelling. No words of encouragement. No cheering on from the outside world. No special foods to support my growth. No strangers' hands on my mother's belly, oohing and aahing, guessing what gender I would be. Just me. Floating around. Quietly creating myself in the dark.

It was good training for a life in show biz. I have often found myself on the road, in some city or country for months at a time, a stranger in a strange land. (FYI, "Stranger in a Strange Land" just happens to be one of my favorite Leon Russell songs, as well as one of my favorite teenage novels by Robert A. Heinlein. Oh, and it also so happens that in Hebrew, "*gershon*" means "a stranger." Fun fact!)

Life as an artist, although sometimes the greatest, can also be isolating and lonely. As one of my great-aunt Ida's many husbands said to me, "Do it for the work, kid, not the glory. It can be a shit life." As I recall, he ended up in jail for embezzlement.

My mother would say to me time and again, "I'm not going to tell you what I think, because you just do what you want anyway." Did she really believe that? Or was this just her way of deflecting guilt for not giving me better advice? Who doesn't want good advice? I crave it, yearn for it, lust after it. You show me a truly wise person and you can bet that I will be right by their side like a hungry little puppy, lapping up whatever crumbs of truth they have to offer.

Still, through the years I've realized that when it comes to important decisions, no one can make those choices but me.

Perhaps I am simply my father's daughter. He always encouraged me to think for myself. And as he grew to trust me and my judgment over the years, I began to trust myself. While some would say follow the money, I have always followed my gut. When I don't, things just seem to go sideways.

Danger in the Trees

Starting at the age of six, my mother decided I was old enough to walk home from school by myself. Things were different then. It seemed to be a more innocent time when a young girl could walk home alone. I was expected to get to school on time, and be home before dinner. No helicopter parenting here. I'd either play board games after school on the playground, go to a friend's house, or, if I didn't have any particular plans, I'd walk home via the Kleins' house. Alan Klein and my big brother, Dann, were best pals; Tracy, my big sister, became friends with Alan's younger sister, Wendy. The oldest Klein siblings—they felt kind of like a young aunt and uncle at this stage. Dann and Tracy were respectively seven and five years older than me, and at my young age of six, that gap felt huge. They had each other to play with, and wanted nothing to do with me. I might as well have been an only child.

Norm and Shirley Klein, the parents, became best friends with my parents and we'd all go away on family vacations together. Balboa Island, Big Bear, and Sequoia National Park for camping. I barely remember those trips since I was like three or four, but I've seen the pictures. While the big kids would go off for adventures, I'd be left behind hysterically crying because I was "too little" to join. I'm sure this is how my "included-out syndrome" took shape. What I do remember with great fondness is the Kleins' refrigerator: Chips Ahoy cookies, Ding Dongs, Ho Hos, fresh watermelon, ice cream sandwiches of the Neapolitan variety, and candy. Lots of candy. Abba-Zabba bars. Snickers. Three Musketeers. Sugar Babies. Almond Joys. Twizzlers. Tootsie Rolls. Pixy Stix. You name it, the Kleins had it. Norm owned a bowling alley in Panorama City, so I guess being fully stocked when it came to goodies was part of his work ethic.

Lubao Avenue, the street on which I lived, was a very long road. At the top of it was Wells Avenue, which was the route I would take coming from the Klein Cantina. As I would turn onto Lubao, there was a cluster of eucalyptus trees to my left. For some reason they scared the shit out of me. I would imagine trolls or ogres or some demonic derelict hiding behind the dark and foreboding thicket of trees, waiting to pounce on me if I got too close. That's why I would always walk on the right side of the street, avoiding potential peril. In fact, one day as I was passing by, I looked straight up the gray and brown peeling trunks into the medicinal-smelling branches, and I swear to you, they spelled out the word *danger*. It was as though Charlotte had moved on from webs to branches. Clear as words on a blackboard:

DANGER. I should probably mention that this was during my witch phase, where I would always search for signs—faces in the gravel, animals in the clouds, demons under the bed, trapped souls in the mirror, what the tinfoil around a Ding Dong would look like after I flattened it with my hand, and if it was secretly trying to tell me something. As if some unfortunate spirit had been imprisoned by an evil tinfoil genie and needed an outsider to help it. Yes, I had a wild imagination, and yes, the only show I would run home to see was *Dark Shadows*, but objectively speaking, those trees really spelled out the word *Danger* if you observed them from a certain angle.

One day, a thirty-something, greasy-haired dude in a powder-blue Chevy Malibu pulled up beside me and asked me the whereabouts of Collins School. I walked a bit closer to the car and helpfully told him there was no Collins School, but that there was in fact a Collier Street School, when I noticed he was butt naked with his hard dick in hand. I didn't lose my cool. I just pretended that nothing was weird and gave him directions to the elementary school he was inquiring about. "Next time I see you, I'm going to shove this up your ass," he told me before speeding off in his car.

I had never seen a naked man before and wondered how his penis could stand up like that. I was also baffled by his threat—was what he told me he was going to do even humanly possible? He must have been confused.

Still, I was scared. I wanted to get home. I had two

very long blocks to go and you can bet when I turned around and saw the powder-blue Malibu coming up behind me again, it felt like a shark zeroing in on its prey. I very calmly and quickly made the decision to walk up to the closest (and unknown) house.

When I turned the handle on the front door it happened to be open, so I just waltzed right in. Luckily for me, there wasn't a guard dog there to attack an intruder. I gave it a few beats, looked outside, and, once the car had passed and was safely down the block, quietly walked out onto the street and ran the rest of the way home.

I pounded on my front door, and as Marie, our housekeeper, opened up, I flung myself into her, wrapping my scrawny arms around her big sturdy knees. I held on for dear life and told her what had happened. Immediately, she said, "We've got to tell Mr. Stan."

"Nooooo," I pleaded. There was no way I could repeat what I saw to my dad. I was still of the age where I was embarrassed to say the word "penis" out loud. But Marie insisted.

Marie had come to live with us when I was two. She would pick me up from school when I was between the ages of four and six because my mom and dad were both working. She would bring me salted carrot sticks wrapped up in tinfoil that were quite delicious. When my parents weren't home and my brother and sister were with their friends, we would eat Cap'n Crunch in big mixing bowls and watch her favorite show on TV—*Roller Derby*.

As we watched, Marie would yell at the TV to

"whoop that white-ass honky." One day, some guy cut my mom off in a car and I yelled, "Look at that white-ass honky!" My mom was not amused and Marie and I got a talking-to. She'd also make me grits, which I loved, and pickled pigs' feet, which I did not. Sometimes Marie had me braid her hair with this stinky linoleum jelly as we watched, and when I got older she made me go to the store to buy her NyQuil for her cough. She'd drink it by the bottle.

Marie was my emotional protector, and her room was my refuge from my relentlessly teasing big brother and sister. I trusted her the most, and would have done absolutely anything for her. One day, my lip bloodied from the effort of trying to play a Jew's harp, which I had just stolen from Thriftimart after seeing Snoopy play one on TV, Marie said, "Child, give me that thing," grabbed it out of my hand, and taught me how to play. She had learned this as a kid on a farm in Rolling Fork, Mississippi, where she was raised. To this day, I've never heard anyone play it better. (Years later, I wrote a song with the great Christian McBride, the best damn bass player in the world, memorializing Marie and my love and respect for her. It's called "Marie." Check it out if you're at all curious.)

Not taking no for an answer, Marie grabbed me by the hand and marched me into my dad's office. I loved the way his office always smelled like cigars. When I reluctantly told him what had happened, mumbling about how the man didn't have any clothes on, my dad took it in and I went back to my room to play, putting the whole incident behind me.

Later that night, my mom and dad called me to the dining room where we had a proper bar. Barstools. Lots of booze. Countertop made out of Spanish tiles. Even an antique cash register that my mom found in London. This was my parents' party spot. My dad liked to make cocktails. His friends liked to drink them. On this night, however, instead of familiar faces, there were two uniformed policemen with pads and pens in their hands, waiting to write down my every word.

I dutifully retold what had happened, but they pressed me for more details. What *exactly* did he show me? I shifted my weight from one foot to the other and kept saying, "You know, you know . . ." looking at my mom, secretly letting her know I wasn't comfortable saying the word out loud in front of two strange men. She nodded to me—egging me on to tell them exactly what I had seen. I guess they needed to hear the actual word for the report.

Finally, after an unbearable silence, I yelled at the top of my lungs, "HIS PENIS!" and ran out of the room. My brother and sister couldn't stop laughing when they heard me scream this at the cops. I, however, was slightly traumatized. There was no comforting from my mother, no coming into my room to see if I was okay.

My parents had done their duty and the right thing by making a report. I just wished it had been handled better. I confronted my mother about this when I was older, after it had come up with my therapist, accusing her of not protecting me, not having my back with those coppers. It was a different time then, as they say. She didn't exactly apologize, she just reiterated that they'd needed it for the report, in my own words, blah blah blah.

A lot of good it did. Within two weeks of the "incident," two young girls were raped on that very street. Fucking Valley. Always had to be on your toes.

Years later—when I was around fourteen, too young to drive, too impatient to walk—I'd skateboard everywhere. I had a shitty wooden board with fancy Cadillac wheels, the best wheels around. Polyurethane and excellent ball bearings had replaced rickety clay wheels by then, making it a much smoother ride on the bumpy street asphalt. I'd get home from school, grab my board, and ride to Carvel ice cream about ten minutes from my house. They had a delightful soft cone that you could get dipped in Oreo-like chocolate crunchies.

I began to notice this beat-up Volkswagen Bug wherever I would go. I wasn't worried, but I definitely clocked it. As I got off my board one day, ready to enter my ice cream haven, an older man with an odd smile on his face came right up to me like some long-forgotten grandpa. He reached out, cupped his hand over my tube top, and shook one of my boobs as if he were shaking the hand of an old acquaintance. I was so shocked—and his friendly demeanor was so baffling—that without thinking, I just knocked his hand away, jumped on my board, and rode straight home. I didn't feel threatened, necessarily, since he was such a frail little thing, but I definitely felt invaded. I couldn't decide if he was a senile old man or a straight-up perv.

For the next bunch of days, his VW was parked across the street from our house. I didn't tell my parents or Marie this time, because I didn't want to repeat the whole police-coming-over-to-the-house-to-question-me sequence, so I would sneak out the side of the house where he couldn't see me, and just stayed aware at all times. After a few weeks, he disappeared.

Little Miss Funtime

When I was six, my parents sent me to Camp Funtime, a day camp that offered many activities such as swimming, horseback riding, and arts and crafts. My brother and sister were off at River Way Ranch Camp, a sleepaway situation. As I was individuating that summer from Little Gigi to Gina, this was a big moment for me. I was really feeling myself. It probably helped that my tormentors (my brother and sister) were away from home and I finally had some breathing room to become my own person.

August arrived and camp was sadly coming to an end. The good news, however, was that there was going to be a talent contest. The winner was to be crowned "Little Miss Funtime" and would get to ride on top of the float at the end-of-summer parade. Who doesn't want to ride on top of a float with a crown on their head? I had to think up something good.

I decided that I would wear my favorite yellow and orange ruffle-bottomed bikini, and play "Born Free" on the piano that my humpbacked teacher had taught me. To jazz it up a bit, I would decorate my skin with my sister's body paint. And to really bring it home, I'd color my belly button green.

My belly button, you see, wasn't just any ordinary belly button, it was an "outie." An outie that protruded from my scrawny little frame about a good half inch. I figured I could ask the counselor to help paint a perfect green square around my meaty little digit and color in the rest. I thought this was truly a genius plan and felt quite pleased about it.

I practiced my piece, put on my bathing suit, then went to my camp counselor to ask for her help. She was around sixteen or seventeen, a typical California blond beauty, and usually very nice and helpful. I handed her the green paint and specific instructions on how exactly to color my belly button. She got down on her knees, faced my extended navel, paintbrush in hand, and began to giggle. The more she painted, the harder she laughed. Soon other girls joined in, pointing at my midsection and crying out: "Look at Gigi's belly button!" Howling laughter all around.

I felt ashamed and embarrassed, but somehow played it cool—not wanting to give these bitchy campers any satisfaction.

I played the shit out of "Born Free," paraded around doing a little dance with my bright-green belly button on display for all the world to see, and actually won. I won that motherfucking contest despite those cunty little girls tormenting me right before I went on. I was crowned Little Miss Funtime. Suck on that, campers.

Not only did I get a sash declaring my new title, but

I also scored a bag of candy and a stuffed animal—a cute little doggie who I named Max.

I felt very proud of my accomplishment, but when I returned from camp and entered our house, I walked straight to my mother, lifted up my shirt, and said, "I want this thing off." I pointed to my jolly-green belly button and in a low, intense, do-not-fuck-with-me-on-this voice stated very clearly, "I. Want. This. Cut. Off."

I wish my mother had talked me out of it. I wish someone had sat me down and enlightened me about the power of individuality, the dignity of not conforming to others' ideas of "normal" or "beauty." The power of loving one's own unique qualities.

But no. Didn't happen. So I had an operation that cut off my beautiful half-inch protrusion of weirdness. And I must admit, I regret it to this very day. I feel horrible that I actually caved to other people's ideas of how I should look.

For better or worse, I think that may have been a catalyst for me not listening to other people's opinions so much. We all get insecure. We all want to look our best and be our best. But really, at the end of the day, it's an inside job. The weird, ugly uniqueness that we all possess makes us individual and beautiful. I'm always attracted to the people who are unapologetically themselves. It's very powerful. It's extremely sexy. Sadly, my belly button is now just a jagged scar, a faint reminder of a lesson learned.

Busted

I was headed off to stay with Aunt Ida and her newly betrothed Ralph in Las Vegas for a long weekend. I've always loved Aunt Ida—she was my own personal Auntie Mame. She wore big sunglasses, a shocking-pink muumuu, a black sequined beanie on top of her platinum-dyed bob, a diamond brooch that spelled *Ida*, and she smoked Virginia Slims out of her signature long, black, and rhinestone cigarette holder. She was maybe four foot ten at best. She picked me up, and within a few minutes we were driving back to her place on a freeway, going against the traffic.

"Oh shit," she cried out, "I think we're going the wrong way!" She pulled onto a ramp as soon as she could and said, "Can you drive?"

"I'm ten," I told her.

"It's as good a time as any to learn!"

I figured I couldn't be as bad as Aunt Ida, and slowly drove us the rest of the way—my feet barely touching the pedals.

When we got to her house, she introduced me to Ralph. He was a slight man—nice-looking face, old as shit, and definitely senile.

As soon as we settled in, my cousin Molly came over. Molly was older—she must've been around sixteen. She was worldly, she'd already had an abortion, and just minutes after arriving, she asked if I wanted to smoke pot. I realized that if I learned how to smoke pot, I'd be one step closer to getting behind the closed doors of my older brother's room where he and his friends were always doing a thing called "bonging."

All I wanted was to be included in my older brother's and sister's activities. My sister Tracy was at that age where she absolutely hated me. She was the coolest person I knew. I was always trying to dress like her—if she had a groovy headband on, I would have to put one on too, or in my case an old piece of red yarn—then she would look at me with disdain and say, "Take. That. Off." We shared a bedroom, wrapped in pink and red floral wallpaper with an old armoire against the wall that my mother had painted white. Tracy drew an imaginary line between our beds and told me, in no uncertain terms, "This is my side of the room, don't ever step in it." The problem was that to leave the room, I had to tiptoe around the perimeter or else I would catch Tracy's wrath, and all I wanted was her love and approval.

So anyway, when Molly offered me the joint, I thought, *Great!*

Next thing I knew, Aunt Ida said, "Hey, girls, I'm going to the casino, please look after Ralph."

That's when the real fun began.

We decided to mess with Ralph's head. I put on

one of Aunt Ida's muumuus, a short blond wig that she had lying around, a sequinned black beanie, her pink lipstick, a pair of her sunglasses, and grabbed her cigarette holder. Then I lay down on her divan upstairs and yelled, "Ralph, Ralph, get up here!"

He wobbled up the stairs and I said in my best Ida voice, "Ralph, get me some water!"

He brought me some water.

"Ralph, get me some grapes, would ya?"

He schlepped downstairs and got me some grapes.

After a few trips up and down the stairs, poor winded Ralph plopped down at my feet, kissed my hand, and wheezed, "Ida, you look younger every day."

When my aunt got back from her casino time, she had bought—as she did almost every day—a box of six chocolate cupcakes. She told me about her winnings, and as we devoured the cupcakes, I told her what had happened with Ralph. She laughed wildly and said, "I'm so happy you had a good time."

The next day, Aunt Ida told me I was ready: she took me to the casino and taught me how to play the slots.

The last day I was there, we went over to Molly's house. It was very hot and everyone was gathered around the pool. Molly and her brother Kurt kept giving me cups of this concoction they had mixed up.

"Here's some punch, Gigi!"

"Have another, Gigi!"

"Look at Gigi, she fell in the pool!"

"Gigi drank all the mai tais!"

I didn't know what a mai tai was, but I did know I'd been pushed in the pool, and stabbed in the back. When my raging headache subsided, I concluded that my cousins were bad news. It was time to leave.

I went home with the confidence of someone who had driven a car, and smoked pot.

As soon as I got back to my house, I called my bestie Lexi and told her it was time to start smoking marijuana—I'd tried it and it was fun, and besides that, her brothers happened to be the main pot dealers of the Valley, so there were literally pounds of marijuana at our fingertips on any given day. So that was when we began smoking every day after school.

Lexi and her brother came by one afternoon and said they had a joint of fresh bud from Hawaii. Maui Wowie. It had red veins running through it and smelled delightful. But where were we to smoke it? My parents were home, so we couldn't smoke there. And it was too hot to go to my fort. So Lexi said, "Why don't we go to Marty's?"

Marty was kind of a hippie, super cool, and she lived across the street from us. I sometimes babysat her kids. Against my better instincts, we went to her house and told her we had a joint. Lexi's brother was older so maybe it seemed okay.

The weed was really strong, and we were laughing our heads off when someone knocked on the front door. Marty got up to answer it, and I heard my mother's voice. She could smell the weed and chuckled knowingly, but when she poked her head through the front door and looked into the living room where we were, she stopped laughing and said, "Oh god, it's my own daughter!"

I jumped up, my arms waving around like a windmill, trying to let her know that everything was fine. She stared daggers at Marty, then turned to me and said, "You're coming with me. We have to go tell your father."

The trip across the street was difficult not only because I knew I was going to get in trouble, but also due to the effects of that special strain. The street was moving as if it were a river—pebbles flowing everywhere, morphing into faces—and I remember thinking, *How do I walk?*

My mom marched me into the room where my father was working, and he looked up and said, "What's going on?"

My mom was right behind me and I just stood there. *Am I supposed to talk? Am I talking now? Who said that?* She nudged me. "Tell him."

Maintain, maintain, maintain, was running through my brain. I said, "Daaaaad"—but I was too preoccupied peering at my father's face. I was so high that his cheeks looked green and had red streams running down them into crevices pooling at his neck. *What a cool way to paint a face*, I thought. He took one look at me and knew. I wasn't able to articulate anything I was thinking, but when he made me promise—before sending me off to my room—that I'd never smoke pot again, I obliged. In my room, I watched pretty shades of red, purple, and green drip down my walls. It was so beautiful . . . until I passed out . . .

The next day, Tracy came into my room and, with an expression of disdain on her face, said, "I heard you got busted."

I tried to be cool: "Yeah."

"I heard you told Dad you'd never smoke pot again."

"Yeah. What else was I supposed to do?"

Tracy looked shocked. Besides being my hero and my fashion inspiration, she was also the voice of reason. She was like the voice of God. She solemnly said, "You lied. You don't lie to Dad."

"What was I supposed to say?"

"You have to tell him the truth."

Oh shit. If Tracy said I had to do it, I had to do it.

Soon thereafter, I found myself in the car with my dad. We were driving through Coldwater Canyon and I had a good fifteen minutes to bring up the subject. I tried: *On the count of three . . . One, two, three . . .* But nothing would come out. *Okay, Gina, you can do this . . . Just say it . . . One . . . two . . . three . . .* I did this probably ten times before finally stammering out a quiet "Dad!"

"Yeah, Bean?"

"Remember when . . . I said I would never . . . smoke again?" The words were coming out like molasses. "Remember when I said I'd never smoke . . . pot . . . marijuana . . . again?" I figured if I talked about it in official terms, I'd sound more serious.

"Yeah."

I blurted out: "I'm sure I will! I bet I will! I'm pretty sure I'm gonna smoke pot again!"

Silence.

More silence.

I'm thinking: *I'm gonna kill Tracy. Fuck fuck fuck!*

After what seemed like an eternity, my dad very calmly, very thoughtfully, replied, "Well, I saw how high you were. I personally do not think you can handle it. I really wish you would wait until you're at least fifteen years old to smoke pot. But I appreciate the fact that you told me because there's nothing you could do that you should ever have to lie to me about. So all I ask of you is that if you have to smoke it, you smoke it in the house."

Whoa. I was dumbfounded. This was not the reaction I'd been anticipating. My dad showed me so much that day—he treated me like an adult. And for that, it was only right that I return the respect. Afterward, I didn't necessarily smoke *in* the house—but I did smoke at the *side* of the house.

The Bully

I am an original Valley Girl—born and raised in Woodland Hills until the precarious age of fifteen, when my parents wisely moved me out of there.

I was, and still am, very affected by my environment and the people I hang out with. I get depressed when surrounded by soul-sucking, uninspired people. *Who doesn't?* you might ask. Many people have an enviable way of maintaining their own emotional state. They do not absorb or get influenced by other people's energies. I, however, for better or sometimes worse, am an empath. I pick up on and internalize others' moods or stress. Once you understand this, perhaps as you grow older, this way of being can be managed and even helpful in reading the room or interpreting what someone is feeling, but for those who do not yet grasp this power, being surrounded by negativity can be challenging.

In the Valley in the seventies, I was submerged in a septic tank of drugs, porn, wasted minds, and pinball machines. It was a potpourri of toxicity, and as I mentioned before, Lexi's big brothers were major pot dealers. There were always pounds of high-class weed in their closet. (We're not talking about the bunk weed that you could buy for ten bucks, we're talking about quality stuff.)

On any given day, Lexi and I would break into her brothers' room, open up their closet, and make the big decision for the day—what should we smoke? Sticky Thai? Colombian? Or perhaps some tasty, veiny bud from Hawaii? It was a simpler time. We didn't know what *sativa*, *indica*, or *hybrid* meant. We just knew one type would get you wasted, another type, more wasted.

We were eleven. My mom was always working and my dad was mostly out of town, and my big sister and brother wanted nothing to do with me. I was basically left on my own. I hung out a lot at Lexi's house. Her mom made the best chicken sandwiches around, her brothers had the best weed, and we were left on our own to get high and raid the refrigerator. Lexi was so sweet and innocent when I first met her. I took it upon myself to show her the way. I schooled her on how to take the white points off her bright new Keds by dragging them along the road going downhill on her bike. For some reason, the pointy toe had to go. Why? I'm not quite sure. It felt a bit too conformist for my taste—reminded me of those *Father Knows Best* ladies I would see on TV with their perfect hairdos and pointy heels that you couldn't run in.

In hindsight, do I wish my parents had insisted on art classes after school or learning a language or perhaps some martial arts? Yes. But the helicopter parent hadn't been invented yet. No one was that interested in what their kids were doing. Sure, my mom drove me to dance classes when I begged her at fourteen, and would take me shopping now and then at the local cute store for teens, Prima Donna, yet I can't help but wonder what would have happened had I been in a different environment. With a little more structure perhaps.

One day as we were walking home—I was going on and on about something or other, so caught up in my story that I didn't realize at first that my bestie wasn't right next to me—I turned around and saw little Lexi with a scared look, tears running down her face.

Stewart Buttsky, an extremely tall and thuggish-for-his-age bully, would not let Lexi pass. Each time she tried to get around him, he would block her with a smug expression on his pimple-riddled face. He always looked smug. Maybe this was due to the fact that he had those big metal braces that constantly cut your lip so you'd have to maneuver your mouth in a way to avoid pain, resulting in a tense, crooked sneer. (I could relate to this later when I, too, had to get the diabolical braces and could barely close my mouth since my lips already protruded upward. Many called me Fishface.)

When I saw my little pal's face all screwed up in anguish and fear, something snapped in me. I went into full Mama Bear mode. I, who had never so much as squashed a beetle, marched right up to Buttsky, tightened my fist into a ball, wound up like I'd seen in the cartoons, and shouted: "Leave my friend alone!"

I slugged the side of his head the way I would hit a tetherball. My aim was impressive, seeing that Buttsky was a good foot and a half taller than me. His face instantly turned beet red, and as he stumbled backward I grabbed Lexi and hollered, "Run!!"

We were both so scared that the Neanderthal would come plowing after us that we didn't stop running, or even look back, until we got safely behind the closed door of my house. I had done what needed to be done in the moment to save my friend, but I knew the consequences might be dire. All I could do was hope that Stewart Buttsky would be too humiliated to tell anyone that he just got whooped by a girl a third his size.

Pinball and Porn

I was around eleven or twelve when I discovered pinball—discovered that I liked it, that I was good at it, and, most importantly, that I could make money from it.

Corbin Bowl had about five pinball machines. To kill time, I would go there after school and play for hours. I desperately needed a change from my usual after-school activities—"playing dead" with my friends or walking through miles of sewage tunnels.

Up until the late seventies, the Valley was full of pomegranate trees and orange groves. To play dead, we'd wear white T-shirts and have pomegranate fights until we were dripping in magenta juice. Then, one of us would lie corpse-like in the street until a car stopped, at which point we'd jump out of our hiding spots, scare the concerned citizen, laugh our heads off, and run away. Other times, we'd try to hit passing cars with flying oranges. Classy. Primo Valley after-school activity. Luckily, we rarely hit our targets.

Then there were the tunnels, which fucking stank. At first we were too dumb to realize they were actual sewage tunnels—we just liked the thrill of holding hands, navigating our way through the pitch dark, and trying to get to a light at the end of the tunnel without being murdered or stepping in shit. Kind of a metaphor for life, I suppose.

The bowling alley was a necessary and welcome change. There was a particular machine called *Swinger*. I liked the way this game was set up. Good, solid, fast flippers. Easy-to-nail bonus points. Bumpers that made a pleasing *ding* when you hit them. Satisfying loops that would light up when the ball raced around them like a speedway. You'd put in a quarter and if you got past a certain score, you'd win a free game. On a good day, I would get up to five free games—hours of mindless, meditative fun.

One time when I was getting frustrated because the ball kept getting stuck, I punched the backboard. I must've hit a sweet spot because all of a sudden it clicked over into another game. I discovered that if I kept doing this, I could get more free games—up to twenty-five of them! I'd then sell those twenty-five games for five dollars—excellent value for a person wanting to play pinball for as long as possible. Usually, my customers would be a group of two or three people who wanted to take turns. I felt I was doing a public service of some sort.

Right next door was the Corbin Theatre that seemed to always be playing *Billy Jack*—the 1971 cult classic film about an ex–Green Beret standing up to corrupt, racist, violent townspeople. It featured that cool antiwar song "One Tin Soldier." The only other way to see films was by getting the Z Channel on cable. The Z Channel was a big deal at that time. I must have watched *Blazing Saddles* when I was sick about a hundred times.

Sometimes after I got done playing pinball, I'd go over and see *Billy Jack*. The only problem was that I couldn't afford to pay for the movie every time I went. With my thrifty spirit, however, I learned how to sneak in. It was pretty simple: I'd go to the back exit and squeeze my nimble little fingers between the doors, push the latch down, carefully press a small button so as not to trigger the alarm, slowly open the doors—not too far because that could also trip the alarm—and slither my way in. I'd gently close the doors behind me and get down on the floor.

Inside, there was a curtain parallel to the screen on the left. I could see the audience from there. I'd sneak past the curtain on my belly, edge into the aisle, and slide into a seat. Then I'd sit up and enjoy the movie.

One afternoon as I was slipping past the curtain, I realized that I didn't recognize the dialogue or any of the sounds that were coming from the screen—a bunch of *ooohs* and *ahhhs*. Hmm. Curious. I peeped out at the audience and glimpsed about twenty men scattered throughout the theater, some of them in raincoats. Seeing as it was pretty hot outside, without a cloud in the sky, I found that very strange. The sounds from the screen intensified, giving way to full-on moaning, groaning, and panting. I didn't recall any of those utterances from *Billy Jack*.

I looked up at the screen and saw a lusty naked

woman caressing a snake. This was definitely not *Billy Jack*. It turned out to be a movie called *The Devil in Miss Jones*. The Golden Age of Porn had arrived.

As fascinated and horrified as I was by *The Devil in Miss Jones*, my attention kept returning to the men in the audience; their flickering glasses reflecting the screen reminded me of fireflies in the night. I decided not to stick around and slithered my way back out of the theater.

Of course, I discussed all this with some of my friends and it soon got around that I knew how to sneak into the theater.

A few weeks later, I was back at Corbin Bowl playing a few games of pinball by myself when Buttsky and his big brother walked in.

After the incident with Lexi, I had learned that Buttsky's big brother was an even douchier dickhead. He treated Stewart the way Stewart treated others—like a little bitch. Bullies get bullied and then become bullies themselves. Good thing to remember.

I tried to act casual, but didn't have my gang with me so I needed to be on my toes. It had been a few years since the head-slugging incident, but payback never comes when you expect it to. The Buttsky brothers didn't ask, they threatened. They had heard I knew how to sneak into the theater, and they told me to take them over and get them in. I had no choice; I didn't want to get my ass kicked. As we headed over, I slyly glanced about to see if there was anyone around who I knew. I was praying that my big brother would drive up in his car right about then.

A few weeks before, my skinny little surfer-boy buddy Derrick, Lexi, myself, and a few other guys were playing touch football in the street. This ninth-grader, who everyone knew was a black belt in karate—because not only did he always tell everyone he was a black belt in karate, but he always wore his gi as a visual reminder—had come up and started bothering us. He grabbed our ball, held it high in the air, and when little Derrick valiantly tried to retrieve it, Karate Guy would laugh and push him away, taunting and humiliating him. The pushes started getting harder and more aggressive until finally I went up to the kid and said, "Leave Derrick alone! Give us back our ball!" At which point, Karate Guy swiftly kicked me roundhouse-style in the stomach. I went flying.

I ran home and told Dann, my big brother, who was prone to violent outbursts on a good day. He was pissed. "Get in the car," was all he said. We jumped into his 240Z and tracked down the agitator. Dann immediately picked the kid up and shoved him against a fence. "If you ever touch my sister again, I'll fucking kill you."

It was a very *Billy Jack* moment. My brother was small for his age and was often bullied growing up. So being able to kick the shit out of someone who was bothering his little sister was definitely in his wheelhouse of justice, not to mention it played right into his fantasy of being a mob boss . . .

But today, at Corbin Bowl, Dann was nowhere to be found. And none of my friends were around for support, either. And there I was with the Buttskys, being forced to do something that I really didn't want to do. I tried to suppress my anxiety. We walked over to the theater and I slipped my fingers between the back doors, carefully holding down the button so as not to trigger the alarm. I told them to be quiet, get down on the floor, inch their way inside, and wait until I closed the door behind me. The older brother crawled inside ahead of me, followed by Stewart. And then, suddenly fueled with anger, I impulsively forced the doors shut behind them—hard enough to trip the alarm. I turned around and ran like hell home. They, on the other hand, got busted.

After that day, my head was like a turret on top of my body. My senses heightened; I would spin around at any sound or peripheral movement, expecting to see the Buttsky boys coming after me with weapons in hand. But they never bothered me again.

Ain't the Marrying Kind

Laura Nelson was a tough old Texas broad who had been my Grandma Peryle's bookie since the 1950s. She was so tough that when her own sister tried to take away young Laura's boyfriend, she waited for the perfect moment for revenge. On the bus ride home from school one day, Laura brought a knife up to her sister's throat and told her that she would kill her if she ever did that again.

"You mess with Laura Nelson, Laura Nelson's gonna mess with you," was her motto.

"Always carry a knife, Geen-Geen," she once told me, "you ain't never gonna know when you'll have to use it."

We pretended Laura was a housekeeper, but housekeeping was not her skill set. Before she would come to the house, my mother would make us tidy up. Laura did make a mean chocolate-pudding pie—she passed the recipe on to me, and to this day I make it for my family every Thanksgiving. Instead of dusting, she would teach me how to play craps and how to talk to the dice. But her real love was blackjack. Her dream was to go to Whiskey Pete's, a casino en route to Vegas, and win four hundred dollars.

One day, when I was playing by myself in the living room, she said to me out of the blue, "Geen-Geen, you ain't never getting married." Marriage was something I heard everyone had to do at some point, so this piqued my curiosity. Marriage meant stability. A house. Someone to take care of you. Family. Did she not think I wanted these things?

I looked up at her and asked, "Why not?"

"You ain't the marrying kind."

At that moment my mother walked in and I told her what Laura had said.

"Oh, Laura, stop talking nonsense."

Of course I'd marry and have kids. I was a nice Jewish girl from the Valley, for Christ's sake.

As my mother was giving me instructions for the day before she headed off to work, Laura mouthed to me behind my mom's back, *You ain't the marrying kind.*

My first memory of Grandma Peryle was when I got to stay over at her house for the night. Just the two of us. I must have been three—whatever age one is when your legs barely jut off a wooden chair. I had to strain to see the top of the kitchen table—that age.

Peryle was teaching me how to play poker. It was time. Five-card stud, classic. I remember thinking that I'd probably be friends with the 4's and 6's, they seemed to be nice. Kind. She told me it was much better to have queens or kings—or better yet, the mighty ace. But it's only 1?? No. She assured me the ace was quite powerful and clever—it could be used for a high or low straight, and they beat out 2's and 3's and even the face cards. The ace of spades looked dangerous, lethal—the secret assassin of the deck.

Did I mention Peryle had a little bit of a gambling problem?

She loved to go to Vegas and play poker. I think it's more than fair to use the word "problem," considering that after she used up all of her own savings, she broke into her children's trust funds and lost it all. The kids today would definitely label her an "addict." But she was a fun lady, a good-time gal who lit up every room. Everyone loved her (except for the woman whose husband she was sleeping with).

Grandpa Chick Gershon, her husband, adored her beyond words. They married and she got pregnant with my father, Stanley. Peryle was a bit wild. She played to the beat of her own tune. She was a passionate woman, a real romantic.

She would fall in love. Hard. So hard that she left the stability of a man who loved her madly—Grandpa Chick—for a crazy time in Vegas with a man she fell head over heels for named Baxter. But eventually, when the money ran out along with the passion (passion, sadly, does seem to have a shelf life), she came back to Los Angeles, had a little whoopsy-daisy with my grandfather, and next thing you know she was pregnant again with my Aunt Bobbi. So she reunited with Chick, and he gladly took her back.

All was kool and the gang for a few years until Peryle started sneaking off to Vegas again, taking some of the family money with her to gamble, and leaving the kids on their own. Grandpa Chick finally had enough and took Peryle to court to gain custody of the kids and finalize a divorce. It was there in court that it was revealed that Aunt Ida and Grandma Peryle weren't even full sisters, but half sisters with different fathers! There was a fight among the five Bronstein brothers in Cheyenne, Wyoming, one of them being Peryle's real father. At some point, and I'm not sure why, the brothers had a huge falling-out, decided to each spell their names differently, and never spoke to one another again. All I know is that when Sharon Stone married Phil Bronstein, we became cousins by marriage.

Anyway, in the last ten years of Peryle's life, well after Chick had died, she was having a salacious affair with another man who happened to be married. She told my parents she didn't care what was happening— no one was to ever come over on Thursdays. At the end of her life—after she had a heart attack and was kept in the hospital—a lovely older gentleman would show up every Thursday with a gorgeous bouquet of roses. When Grandma Peryle died, it was the first time I had ever seen my dad cry. We all went away to Big Sur for some family healing time, and my brother to this day swears that in the middle of the night Peryle appeared next to me, bent over and gave me a kiss goodbye, smiled at him, and then vanished.

Years later, when I was living in New York City—

where I always carried a knife, per Laura Nelson's advice—I thought it would be great to take Laura on a road trip to Whiskey Pete's. She could tell me all the secrets and stories about Peryle that only she knew. Sadly, a few weeks before our adventure was to occur, Laura had a stroke and could no longer speak. All she could do was smile and laugh at me when I'd ask her questions about Peryle, my family, myself. Laura died not long after that, and was buried with Peryle's secrets.

I remember one very hot, muggy summer in New York City when my AC broke. For those of you who have lived through the sweltering, oppressive heat of a summer in the city, you can appreciate what a disaster this is. No AC during July and August is just not a civilized option. Unfortunately, my bank account was also a bit broke. I needed around six hundred bucks to buy a new cooling system. I thought to myself, *WWLND?* (What would Laura Nelson do?) So I hopped on a bus for a day trip to Atlantic City for a little gambling. I felt Grandma Peryle by my side the whole time, cheering me on. When I was up $675 at the craps table, I called it a day, headed back to the city, and bought a decent air conditioner the next morning. I could feel the pride of Peryle, and I could see Laura's happy face, laughing with approval.

And to this day, for better or worse, I have yet to marry.

The Fort and the Football Player

My first fort was across the street in the underbelly of an enormous fig tree. If you pushed aside one of the many low-hanging branches, you would find a cavernous haven inside that protected you from the heat and annoyance of the outside world. I remember my other grandmother on my mom's side, Estelle, making jars and jars of jam with the ripe figs that would fall heavy and purple from the tree.

I would allow my chosen people into my private sanctuary for various reasons. My girl gang, called the Sly Foxes, consisted of my four best friends—Lexi, Alex, Kristy, and Sherry—and of course they were always welcome. Here, we would conduct official after-school meetings, discussing whatever was of the utmost importance at that particular moment: *Should we all twin every day, or just on Wednesdays? Which boys are cute? Who would you secretly like to kiss? What's the best way to eat an Abba-Zaba bar without one of your braces coming out? What games should we play at the slumber party next weekend?* You know, the important stuff when life was simple.

There was something very regal and grand about

sitting on my rock, addressing whatever needed to be addressed, casually reaching up to pluck a big fat purple fig, slowly, delicately, almost sensually peeling back the skin to expose the white pith surrounding the textured, juicy interior. It made me feel like I was some ancient queen conducting the people's business. All I was missing was a scepter.

Several years later, when kissing fantasies and small talk had evolved, the fort became our love den—a place to make out with our designated partner. Gone were the days when we would get "drunk" off of Manischewitz wine at bar mitzvahs and tease each other shamelessly; we had now graduated to full-on groping.

One day, I walked into my safe haven to have a little alone time and was startled and then horrified to see it strewn with *Playboy* and *Penthouse* magazines, a few crushed beer cans, and crumpled tissues all over the place. Someone had infiltrated and sullied my fort—the violation sickened me with anger.

Everyone knew this was *my* fort. I had lived across the street from it my entire life and had claimed it as my own. I had a sneaking suspicion that it might've been the new guy who recently moved down the block. He was tall, lanky, and a little bit older. I didn't know him at all, but my Spidey instinct told me it was him. I cleaned up his mess and went on with my business.

And then it happened again. I saw the new guy on the street the next day and told him that the fig-tree fort he was defiling was *my* fig-tree fort and that he needed to stay out of it. He didn't deny anything, he simply stood there looking down at me. He must've been in the eighth or ninth grade, and he just kind of laughed it off and walked away. I was nice about it, but pretty firm.

After my friendly neighborly warning, however, the guy kept right on violating my sanctuary and I got increasingly pissed. One afternoon, there was a game of touch football on our street and he was the quarterback. I was on the opposite team and my job was to rush the quarterback. My rage quickly boiled up and as soon as he said "Hike," I found myself flying through the air, aiming to tackle the shit out of him. I succeeded in knocking him to the ground, but managed to smash my nose on the cement road in the process. With blood running down my face, adrenaline pumping through my body, I yelled, *"Stay the fuck out of my fort!"*

I probably seemed a little crazy, sure, but from that day forward he stayed the fuck out of my fort. He knew I meant business.

Sleepovers

We were bored. We were antsy. There wasn't much for us to do in the Valley that didn't include some sort of delinquent activity. Stealing. Bombing innocent bystanders with water balloons. Smooshing eggs in people's mailboxes. Usual dumb shit.

Both my parents were working. My mom would drive me to the occasional volleyball tournament or dance class, but mostly I was on my own. I'd leave the house for school and come home at dinnertime. I don't really recall any discussion of *What did you do after school?* or *How was your day?* My parents cared that I stayed out of trouble, made my curfew, and got A's. That was about all that was required of me.

The Sly Foxes had a whole secret language—little symbols we made up for letters like some ancient Egyptian code just in case anyone found our notes. We had many sleepovers where we'd stay up all night telling ghost stories and exchanging secrets. Raiding the refrigerator for snacks late at night was a sleepover favorite—we called it "Stealing Food." Technically, we weren't really *stealing*—more like sneaking—but the name gave it a clandestine feel, making the task at hand all the more exhilarating to young adrenaline junkies such as ourselves. Before stealthily returning to our slumbers with our stash, we had to rearrange the refrigerator to cover our tracks and not cause any suspicion the next day.

This skill came in handy years later when I was in college and could barely afford two meals a day, let alone kitchen supplies. It's a struggling actor's instinct to gather and save free food when it's around. At any event with free food, there would usually be a way to snag some of it and save it for later. And while you were at it, some cutlery might be nice. I had an actor friend once who expertly stuck a teapot in his backpack at some fancy benefit because he needed one at home and couldn't afford to buy it. Impressive.

As for myself, when my Uncle Jack, who was a jazz musician, had a show to arrange and conduct and he and my aunt were in town staying at some posh hotel courtesy of whatever network had hired him, I would visit and casually take any forks, knives, spoons, or coffee mugs left on room service trays in the hallway. I'm not too proud to admit that if there was an untouched bread basket, I'd nab those contents as well. I have friends today—successful friends—who will steal a napkin or two from their favorite restaurant until they have a set. They are probably just kleptos—but regardless, our "Stealing Food" game was good preparation for my early years as a hungry young actor in New York City.

So back to our sleepovers.

We were young girls dreaming about having boyfriends one day. After the lights went out, once we were done eating our stolen goods, we would pass the pillow around and show how we would make out with our future beloved. A few times we brought out the flashlight to check out each other's vaginas up close.

"Ohhh, look, it's like a weird cave—kind of like a tunnel!" We called this game "Exploring." The explorer would issue reports as her fingers mined through uncharted territory. Then she would pass the flashlight to the next girl to explore her own secret quarry. We thought our vaginas were funny. They made us laugh. Sometimes they would even have conversations like they were dolls and we were ventriloquists. We were getting to know our bodies without shame or embarrassment—just curiosity.

One day after school, my friend Sherry grabbed my hand and urgently told me she needed to show me something. We went to her house, where she led me to her bathroom, locked the door, and proceeded to run a bath. I whined that I didn't feel like taking a bath this early in the day. She told me to shut up and trust her. She didn't fill the tub very far and asked me to get in and hold her head up so her hair didn't get wet. She was practical that way.

I held her head in my hand as she placed her legs up on her tiled wall and let the warm stream fall between her legs like a miniwaterfall from the gods.

"What are you doing?" I asked her. I didn't get it—it seemed dumb.

"I can't really explain it," she whispered back, eyes closed, "but this *thing* happens . . ."

Sure enough, after a few moments her face started to screw up—she wiggled around and made little squeaky noises that were just on the edge of laughter. I remember peering at her upside-down face and how her dark, straight eyebrows suddenly looked like her mouth and her whole face had changed. Her ears were basically in the same place, grounding her new face in a strange and realistic way. Her mouth was one elongated eye—like some friendly cyclops. As I was contemplating this new breed of human, Sherry let out a high-pitched squeal, gasped, and jolted up—bringing her legs down hard, as if someone had punched her in the gut.

I asked her if she was alright, and she said, "WHHHOOOOAAAAAAA!" She seemed a bit dizzy, but breathlessly told me that I had to try it. "It feels sooooo good," she insisted.

We started going to her house—and her bathtub—every single day after school. We'd walk in, Sherry would say, "Hi, Mom, we're home!" and we'd casually saunter off to the bathroom. Then we'd lock the door and take our bath.

We had no idea what an orgasm was. We started calling it the "Thing." "Let's go do the Thing!" It was sweet and innocent and ultimately empowering. We knew how to make ourselves feel good. We knew what we liked. We were ready to take it on the road, as they say.

To Thine Own Clit Be True

It was around this time that we started getting crushes. Truth or Dare was introduced to our Friday-night parties. Spin the Bottle felt too random. Sure, there was the obvious cheap titillation of exhibitionism amongst peers, but the real raison d'être—who would kiss who—was planned out and discussed way before the party even began. Much of this centered around Alex and me thinking Grant was hot. We both wanted to kiss him.

Alex (who was at this time the only other girl who had boobs) and I had decided it was time to "go steady" with someone. We chose Bob and Dean to be our paramours. Alex leaned toward Dean, and I was cool with Bob—I just liked the idea of going steady. I had read about it in my sister's diary; anything she was doing, I wanted to do as well, even if I didn't totally understand the concept.

We made a plan: after recess, we would tell Dean and Bob that we were going steady. There wouldn't be any asking involved—we would just let them know what was up. I told Alex that before informing the guys of our new relationship status, we each had to get rings to make it official. So I rode my bike to the turquoise lady on Ventura Boulevard and carefully picked out two rings. One for me, one for Bob. Simple and classy. Silver and turquoise. Four dollars and fifty cents each.

When Bob and I broke up two weeks later, I took my ring back and, I kid you not, still have it to this day.

Now that Pandora's box was open, we wanted more. Every week I seemed to have a new crush on a different boy. If you read my journal entries during that period, they would go something like this:

Dave Douszner. 14. Surfer boy. A total babe.
Kevin Jones. 14. Super cute but kind of a douche. I'd still like to kiss him.
Oh my god!!!! SCOTT MCCROCKIN!! So HOT!! 16!!! He doesn't say much. He doesn't need to. I am totally in love with him!!!!!

And so on and so on. I was still young enough to think that "quiet" meant "mysterious and knowing," instead of, more likely, "potentially dumb without having anything to say." I learned this later on in life, in my twenties, when that sort of thing made a difference.

Truth or Dare quickly became a crowd favorite at all the parties. You'd tell your best friend who you wanted to kiss, and then when it was her turn, she would ask you the proverbial question, "Truth or dare?" You'd choose "dare," knowing that it would lead to making out with your secretly chosen crush. Then, of course, there was the making out in the center of a circle, unleashing torrents of passion in front of your classmates.

I mean, it's weird to be intimately engaged in front of a crowd of spectators. You have to blot them out and concentrate solely on your partner without getting self-conscious. Truth or Dare was excellent training for the professional love scenes I'd be doing later. Although I must say, and I'm sure you've heard this before, doing a love scene is not that sexy. It's very technical. You have to be aware of the camera and the choreography of the scene, and you can never lose sight of whatever emotion your character is feeling or why this is happening in the first place. Sometimes it's a barometer into who your character really is.

My very first love scene was in *Cocktail*. I got lucky: my partner was Tom Cruise and he could not have been sweeter or sexier. We definitely had chemistry and I couldn't believe I was getting paid to make out with him. Originally, the scene had us running naked around the hot tub until we started kissing. But that just seemed gratuitous and lame.

I suggested that Tom start covertly, underneath the covers. Then he could pop up and, surprise, he's been going down on me. It would be a nice reversal of what we usually witnessed in the movies. Tom loved the idea, so that's what we did. I couldn't have asked for a more supportive and communicative and trustworthy partner. He even suggested that I turn away so that my breasts weren't on camera, just facing him. I believe I proposed that he cover them with his hands just to be sure. I may be making this up; I can't remember exactly. During one take, he started tickling me. I had warned him about tickling—I go crazy and can't control my actions. He didn't take me seriously, I guess, and I ended up kneeing him in the face at the beginning of the scene. I thought I had broken his nose. I apologized profusely. I felt terrible. But Tom, the eternal gentleman, said he was okay and acknowledged that he'd been warned. We carried on.

Sometimes you aren't so lucky. Sometimes you have a scene with an acting partner who seems okay at the beginning of the shoot, and then when the story calls for some intimacy, the mere thought of kissing this person makes you want to puke. You think to yourself, *Oh God, I really have to do this? Because the scene requires it? Because I'm getting paid? What am I, a prostitute?* You have to find a way to make it work—either shifting the kiss to a neck instead of a mouth, using the old substitution technique, or doing all sorts of psychological gymnastics. In other words, you gotta *act*. Luckily, this has only happened to me twice in my career. And no, I will not tell you who—because as I said from the beginning, this is not that kind of book and I'm not that kind of girl. Maybe if you get me drunk . . .

At least in Truth or Dare, if you are dared to kiss someone you loathe, you can always switch over to "truth."

* * *

Grant and I held the record for kissing the longest—ten minutes straight. (We were timed.) Sometimes we would enhance our session by sucking on watermelon or apple candies for that little extra something. I personally loved a hot cinnamon treat before going at it, but you always had to ask for consent on that one. Some people aren't comfortable if things get too spicy.

When it was time to try second base, Grant and I thought it should be in private so we made a separate plan. He met me at my house and we went over to my trusty fort, where we promptly started to make out. When he awkwardly tried to put his hand down my shirt, he got tangled in my little fish necklace that my father had given me, so I suggested he go *up* my shirt instead. We figured it out.

Alex and I would sometimes even share Grant. No jealousy or weirdness, just curiosity, trust, and fun. Did that make us a throuple?

A few years later, when Grant and I were at separate schools—he went to Portola, I went to Parkman Junior High—he called and told me that he'd had actual sex the night before. He had been seduced by an older woman! Grant was gorgeous and cool, so I wasn't surprised. When I asked him how it was, he said it was great although he had no idea what he was doing when it came to oral sex. How would he know? I definitely didn't have a clue. We agreed that we needed to figure it out.

The next day, I told my mom I was going over to Grant's house to do some homework. We took turns going down on each other, exploring, telling each other what felt good and what didn't. My bathtub experiences with Sherry gave me a few clues on how to guide him. It was a healthy, wonderful relationship that prepared me for all things oral in the real world. It was very innocent and constructive and it helped me get to know and respect my body. It makes me sad when I hear girls in their twenties and thirties talking about being engulfed in hookup culture and thinking they are liberal feminists because they can have sex "like a man." What does that mean exactly? Pursue, woo, win, cum, and go? No emotional attachments, just hooking up, getting off, or in most cases for the girls, *not* getting off, then on to the next? Personally, that has never been very satisfying or fulfilling. Too often it seems these girls are left sexually frustrated and disappointed. Why fake an orgasm? I faked an orgasm once because I just wanted the sex to be over—I had never really intended to sleep with the guy, whom I liked and respected. But I was stoned and my body and brain were in two different places, having two different conversations.

Mind: *Why are we doing this? I don't want to have sex with this guy.*

Body: *Well, how do we stop?*

Mind: *Not sure. This will be weird. Let's just get this over with, then get out of here.*

So that's what we did. The guy seemed hurt that I wanted to leave so quickly. We never should have had sex!! Not his fault. Mine. Definitely not a very AlphaPussy move. I was around twenty-two when this occurred and I learned to never again get high with a man alone in his house unless I knew him *very* well and was totally comfortable saying NO to him if anything felt strange. A good lesson anyway and always.

I refuse to party and make myself vulnerable in that way, unless I am around people I trust so I can have wild fun knowing I am safe and protected.

The McMansion

It was one of those hot, smoggy days in the Valley. The kind of day where the air is so bad they cancel PE. The kind of day that by the time you walk from the bowling alley back to your house, you feel like a zombie. So hot that your head feels swollen and your words come out slowly, as if your mouth is full of Jif peanut butter. Lexi and I were trudging home when we were approached by a few local guys. We'd seen them around but certainly weren't close with them. They asked if we wanted to come over and smoke a joint. One of the guys' houses was down the street, at the end of a cul-de-sac. I recognized it—I'd always wondered what the house with the golden arches looked like inside. (Rumor had it that they owned the McDonald's chain, thus the golden arches.) I figured if they were rich, they'd probably have decent weed, and it was boiling-hot out. So, even though I didn't know them well, we said sure, why not—AC, weed, a Coke . . . no one needed to twist our arms.

The house was big and kind of ugly—I guess you could call it a McMansion. It had smooth marble floors and high gray walls, with a bunch of hallways spidering off to different rooms, all connecting at the center of the house where a tacky gold water fountain stood—a cheap, miniature version of the beautiful marble ones that I would later witness all over Rome. The sound of the water coming out of the fountain echoed through the hallways, emphasizing the vast emptiness of the expensive residence. It felt cold, unused, soulless. The parents of the guy who lived there must have been away; in any event, no one else seemed to be around as we made our way to Ron's room. (I can't really remember his name so let's just call him that.)

Ron's bedroom was pretty huge, more like a suite. It had its own mini living room attached to it, a fancy-looking bed tucked away in the far corner, and an adjoining bathroom. More importantly, he had his very own pinball machine. I'd never seen that before. These guys must be *really* rich, I thought, and immediately asked if I could play. We gathered around the machine and started to battle it out against each other. One of the boys pulled out a joint and we passed it around.

As I took a hit, an unusual, harsh chemical taste slightly burned the inside of my mouth. Whoa. Head rush. Very dizzy. I saw explosions of light, bright flowers blooming in the sky like it was the Fourth of July. My hands gripped the sides of the machine, the flipper buttons acting as a sort of lifeline. Next thing I knew, I was on a ship. Bells clanging. Sails whipping. The sea roaring. My fingers, now detached from the rest of my body, were in charge of keeping the engine running. I was like a little mouse on a big ship, scurrying about, trying to survive the ferocity of the swell, avoiding the stampeding boots of the frantic seamen, the clanging of the bells warning me of danger—*Keep running, little mouse, watch out! Get out! Get out! Get out!*

I wasn't quite sure how much time had gone by, but now I was back in the room, still clutching the pinball machine. Where was Lexi?

I asked one of the guys and he told me he thought she was in the bathroom. I made my way over, walking as though my legs were made of lead, and there was my friend—totally wasted, giggling hysterically on the bathroom floor. Two of the other boys were in there as well—one sitting on the sink, the other leaning against a wall—expressionless, watching Lexi on the floor laughing like a crazy person.

Now, you have to understand, Lexi and I had been smoking weed every day. With her brothers being dealers, we were by now seasoned stoners. I quickly recognized that something was off; we were high in a different sort of frequency. A buzz with which I was not familiar. I had heard stories about people lacing joints with angel dust. Even in my haze, I wondered if we had been dosed. Then, out of the corner of my eye, I saw one of the guys pulling the sheets back on Ron's bed. Alarm bells began to go off in my head: we needed to get out of there.

I said to Lexi, "Hey, we have to go meet your mom."

"No we don't," she singsongily replied.

She was stupid high.

"Lexi, we need to go." I gave her a pointed look as I grabbed her arm and flicked my eyes over to the undressed bed—the guy standing there next to it as if waiting for us to be delivered to him. Another guy was still at the pinball machine, and the two in the bathroom now looked quietly menacing.

I yanked Lexi's arm and somehow made her understand that we needed to get the fuck out of there. It seemed like the guys were starting to get annoyed. I felt desperate, but acted polite as I dragged a stumbling Lexi toward the front entrance.

"No, you can't go," one of the boys said.

I pretended not to understand what was going on—a tactic I've deployed for years to avoid making threatening men get more aggressive. I feigned silliness, sweetness, and naivete. (I will also maintain that I could've beat these scrawny fellows in a fair fight. Well, maybe not, but the drugs imbued me with false bravado.)

As I pulled Lexi along, I heard one of the guys say, "I guess you were more into Billy." I didn't understand what he meant, but all I cared about was getting away, fast. *Get out, get out, get out, little mouse!*

There was just one remaining problem: I couldn't for the life of me figure out how to get out of the McMaze. I kept dragging Lexi back to the fountain, and the sound was so loud and disorienting now that we kept making wrong turns through doorways and couldn't find the front door.

I don't know how I kept my wits about me in that

moment. If it were up to Lexi, we would have just laid down on the cool marble floor. She was getting sluggish and tired now. How much of that shit did she smoke? Knowing Lexi, a lot.

Eventually, somehow, we found those enormous front doors. They seemed like they were made of concrete—but finally, once opened, we ran out, down the cul-de-sac, and onto the streets of Woodland Hills. The air was still very hot and dry, but we semi-sprinted all the way home, and passed out upon arrival.

Later on, we found out that the "Billy" I'd heard one of them mention in the McMansion was the same douche who I'd tackled for infiltrating my fort. He had gone around lying about how me and Lexi would "put out" for weed. It turns out—and there were many such cases, as life went on—that guys like Billy don't appreciate a girl whooping his ass, so like a little, sneaky, cowardly wimp, he'd tried to hurt me in other ways. What a chump.

Thrifty Balls

My first real paying job—if you don't count dancing as a spirit for my sister, aka Madame Tracy (more on this later)—was at a place called Chicken Shirt when I was about twelve. It was a T-shirt shop where customers would pick a decal (anything from a sleepy kitten to a gnarly wave to a good ol' *Keep on Truckin'* logo), choose a shirt color, and I'd press the design on with a giant heat machine. Hopefully straight. Usually not. Voilà—custom fashion magic.

Chicken Shirt was within walking distance of our house, in a Ventura Boulevard minimall that had absolutely everything: Abe's Deli, a hardware store, the local record shop, a dry cleaner, and my personal fun house—Thriftimart.

Now, "steal" might be too harsh a word. I took gum from Thriftimart, sure—but it was technically free with a purchase. And I had *thoughts* about purchasing—god knows my family had purchased tons in the past. So let's call it a moral limbo. Either way, the thrill was real. Plotting my petty heist, slipping the gum into my pocket, making the clean getaway—it gave my restless little brain a reason to spark. A cheap shot of dopamine in the otherwise blank void of aimless afternoons.

I wish I'd had something better to channel all that energy into. The kids I ran with weren't particularly inspired—or inspiring. We didn't paint, or sing, or write, or do much of anything. That kind of nothing turns into trouble. And trouble thrives where there's no supervision, no purpose, and too much time to kill.

I wasn't one of those naturally self-starting types. I needed friction, collaboration—some spark. A sound, a movement, a moment of eye contact with someone I connect to on a primal level. Almost like the recognition of a tribal member who sees us as we really are. And acknowledges our true essence. I've always believed we're born with wild colors inside us, but life, over time, shades them with an invisible black crayon. Then, every once in a while, someone or something scratches the surface—and the buried color reveals itself once again.

This was all before I discovered organized sports and after I'd aged out of the monkey bars. The streets became our playground. We egged houses. We broke fluorescent tubes in the road just to hear them pop. We raced dirt bikes through the canyon. We "stole" gum, candy, anything that wasn't bolted down. And eventually—when the thrill of stealing what was free wore off—we graduated to the real stuff. First it was yo-yos. Then records. Then, one super-ambitious day, a bicycle. Okay, it belonged to a kid I knew, and it was just that one time, but the rush of sneaking it out from under his nose was quite satisfying. I felt like a rebel queen riding home, wind in my braids, a stolen crown between my hands.

When the guy finally showed up to claim his bike (some punk must have squealed on me), I gave it up graciously. He called me a bitch—the first time that ever happened—and even though I didn't like that he said it, I saw the logic behind his anger and secretly thought . . . *Fair*. I didn't steal anyone's bike after that.

I'm not an asshole. I was just passing the time.

One day, one of my besties was coming over to play. Our game at the moment was tossing a small ball back and forth without dropping it, trying to beat our latest count. I believe we were up to 117 passes. Much to my dismay, I realized that I was out of balls. Must have lost them in the street throwing them at some target—a sign or mailbox—when we had run out of eggs. Shit.

It wouldn't be cool if Suzy came over and I didn't have what was necessary to break our own record. I was in our pool when I realized that I'd have to go down to the store and get a few balls before my guest arrived. I didn't really feel like getting out of my suit, it was one of those super-hot Valley days. So I just threw my little knitted cape over my wet bathing suit. I've always loved a cape—so mysterious and sophisticated—and to be honest, I figured it would be a perfect cover for the merchandise I was planning to lift.

I got on my purple Schwinn—complete with a floral banana seat, sissy bar, and peace sign on top—and rode down to Thrifty's. Once inside, down aisle number 4, I was delighted to see that they had restocked my play section. So many balls! So many different pretty colors! How was a gal to choose? I really liked the blue and red ball. But I thought the shocking-pink and green ball was super cool. And how could I turn away from the bright-orange and hot-pink orb of rubber? Oh, and the black one with silver stars was exceptionally groovy. I absolutely could not make up my mind—so I committed one of the oldest crimes known to the downfall of mankind . . . I got greedy. I took them all. I was in my cape, after all. Easy-peasy.

As I was walking out the door with my loot carefully clasped in my grubby mitts, I felt a hand on my shoulder, and then a police badge flipped dramatically in front of my face.

I flashed on the sign in the window that I'd never noticed before—*SHOPLIFTERS WILL BE PROSECUTED*—and was immediately annoyed with myself for not having paid attention to that warning. It was quite literally a sign telling me that I should have been more careful. I had been too cavalier! Amateur!!

As we did the perp walk to the back of the store, I saw the mom of one of my friends and had to act like everything was okay so as not to raise suspicions that I was now a hardened criminal. After all, if I was a convicted felon, that would mean no more playdates with her daughter.

Once we were in the back room, I pleaded with the cop not to call my parents. I even offered to bring him back ten dollars—double the price of the stolen balls. I didn't say he could pocket the extra five bucks, but that was implied. "Bribery" was a word not included in my limited vocabulary, but I instinctively understood the concept. He just chuckled, twisted his cliché cop 'stache, and looked away as though he was thinking how funny this story would be to tell later at the bar with his cop buddies.

I felt humiliated.

The cop called my parents and they told me to come home. Immediately. On my ride of shame home, I kept trying to think of what excuse to use—but I just couldn't find one. Needless to say, I was grounded for weeks.

I'll never forget the looks on my parents' faces when they said, "We are so disappointed." Their reaction was devastatingly effective. And the fact that they didn't yell at me somehow made it worse. That's something I noted later when I was making acting choices—the calmer you are, the more effective the blow. I felt horrible and hollow inside as I accepted my punishment and walked to my room—head hanging low. My career as a master thief ended that fateful day.

Baseball and Boobs

I had just turned fourteen and my mother insisted I get a bra.

Prima Donna was my mom's go-to store in the Valley, and we'd often head there together on girls' days. Get some lunch, have a heart-to-heart, shop. That was our jam. For the last few years my wardrobe had consisted mainly of Hang Ten shirts, Dittos jeans, and Keds sneakers. Every now and then I'd find a random T-shirt with Woodstock from *Peanuts* on it, or some other cute animal—a teddy bear, Winnie-the-Pooh, etc.—but my main look always had a pair of feet, ten toes, and a cool insignia.

On this day, however, we walked into Prima Donna and I saw a tight, cream, knit sweater that I just loved. I thought it would look amazing with my new Chemin de Fer high-waisted jeans, a perfect outfit for Friday nights at the roller rink. My mom pointed out my newly budded breasts and insisted that I wear a bra with this form-fitting top.

I didn't necessarily want boobs—I liked the way clothes fit without a chest. Little titties were fine and pretty, yet they threatened to grow into actual boobs and, god forbid, a bosom. Too big for me. But the main reason I was against boobs and a bra was that I didn't think the guys would take me seriously anymore.

My friend Alex and I were the resident tomboys of our friend group. Alex knew what was going on. She hung out with the cool Black kids and they showed her the groovy new dances—then she'd teach me. We would all meet in the girls' bathroom to perfect our moves. Alex was also developing boobs that she hid under large T-shirts. What were we to do? We were both really good athletes—we played baseball, football, and Sock-o with the boys. We were competitive and the boys respected our skills.

Sock-o involved dividing into two teams and playing on hard ground, with goalies on each side. It was a fast-paced, gnarly game. The object was to throw the ball as hard as you could at one of your opponents, beaning them in the gut, head, ankle, or, well, anything goes. Your opponent, however, if they were stealthy, could dodge the ball or, better yet, catch it, pivot, and throw it back at you to try to get you out.

We all had our signature Sock-o moves that we became known for. Alex had sheer power and aim, Dean had this incredible ability to catch just about everything, and Bob could dodge anything—even if the ball was thrown right at him from a foot away. And then there was me . . . Well, I became known as "Spider Legs," and not just because of my tight lowrider Dittos. (Look it up: they were super-cute jeans in that era—I was really into the inch-long zipper and flair just below the knee, and such an array of colors! I really think that Dittos would be a big hit now. Someone should start making them again.) I was very skinny then, and my Sock-o superpower was that I could straddle-jump over the ball and not get hit. It was an oddly instinctual move, and had real flash appeal.

That day at Prima Donna, my mom finally convinced me to buy a bra. It was time. Soon thereafter, as I had feared, everyone started noticing that I had boobs. And all of a sudden everyone wanted to see them.

One day on the playground, a group of boys approached me and said they'd give me five dollars if I walked across the playground with my top off. Momentum gathered, and soon a few more kids, girls included, were throwing money at my feet.

I was like, "No, I'm not gonna do that!" It was upsetting.

The next thing I knew, the whole playground seemed to swarm around me, pushing me, coercing me to take off my top. Demanding that I walk from one end of the playground to the other, topless, obeying their commands.

I tried to play it cool, laugh it off, but I was fucking dying inside. There was an unspoken power-dynamic shift: I had something they wanted. But it wasn't something I wanted to give them. My will against theirs. They were like a pack of wild animals. Shouting. Snarling. Eyes flashing. It was scary. It was intense. So I did the only thing that occurred to me in the moment: I just snickered like this was all beneath me, flipped my hair back, and sauntered away.

I was a pretty solid baseball player. I could really connect when I swung the bat, and had a great arm. I mean, I was no Shohei Ohtani, yet I could certainly hold my own. But boobs fundamentally altered my relationship to the game and my fellow teammates. When guys saw me with a tighter top and boobs, their attitude toward me definitely changed.

Now, when I stepped up to the plate, the boys would get shifty eyes—stammering and mumbling. They were no longer respecting my game. It's as if they thought boobs were stopping my swing from being able to hit a double or triple.

I also noticed that the tighter my tops got, the stupider guys became. I didn't know if they were moving in closer just to see my shape, or if they seriously thought I couldn't hit anymore. This was annoying, so I leaned into it. I would lamely swing "like a girl with boobs," and they'd step a little bit closer.

Strike!

I'd swing again: miss.

They'd come in again: strike!

And when they came so close that I knew I could easily knock it over their heads, I'd swing, hit the ball, and run around all the bases, flipping them off in my mind as I'd complete my home run.

Years later, I would use this technique when I was playing in the Broadway Show League. Since the

1950s, the Broadway Show League has been a tradition, where different teams representing each show play softball against each other in Central Park. The teams usually consist of the tech people, crew members, stagehands, a few actors, and anyone else affiliated with the show. Ironically, when I was actually appearing in Broadway shows, *Cabaret* and *Bye Bye Birdie* specifically, I was too paranoid about injuring myself, since I'd be singing and dancing and generally needed to rest up during the day. But before that I was recruited to play on several teams, since they were required to have at least two girls per team (if memory serves).

If we were playing against a new team, I'd wear a very tight baseball top representing the show, pretend I couldn't hit, watch them move closer, and then smash the ball over their heads. This would only work once, obviously, before the other team understood I was a player. Sometimes it is very satisfying to be underestimated.

One of Our Cheerleaders Is Missing

As a young actress—still in high school, before I had an agent—I used to scour the pages of *Backstage* looking for jobs. The magazine kept a list of castings for movie, TV, and theater. It would describe the part—something like, "Looking for a willowy, blond, innocent, soft-spoken girl, sixteen to twenty years old, daughter of a preacher, knows how to twirl a baton a plus . . ." or, "White, male, athletic type, captain of the football team who is harboring dark secrets . . ." etc.—and then offer information on who to contact.

I was anxious to start working. I really wanted to act in movies. I was doing school plays as well as taking drama and dance classes. I thought I was ready to go pro.

Truly, I wasn't. But my enthusiasm was real. So every Friday I would buy this trade magazine and attempt to begin my career. Who needed an agent?

One day I came across a listing that sounded super promising: "Searching for a female who looks like she's in high school, has leadership qualities, attractive, athletic figure, fierce, smart, tough, flexible, dancing or gymnastics abilities a plus. Must be eighteen or older." I thought: *Hey, I'm all those things! I'm perfect for this!*

Well—except for the eighteen-or-older part. I was fifteen at the time but I *looked* older. I had a fake ID (just like all the other Valley kids in those days) and was used to lying about my age. I figured the actress had to be at least eighteen so that she could work more hours without a required teacher. Whatever. I thought I was made for the part. I was a dancer and a gymnast! I was fierce and tough! This part was mine! I sent in my résumé and headshot.

A week later, I got a response in the mail that said:

Thank you for responding to what is now titled, One of Our Cheerleaders Is Missing. *This is a very demanding role. A real tour de force. Our hero, a cheerleader who has been kidnapped, has to be able to play fear, toughness, vulnerability, cunning, terror, all while tied to a brick wall. She needs to manipulate her captor by pretending to be into him, all while planning her escape. I will not only be directing, writing, and editing this cutting-edge film, I'll also be acting the role of the "Deranged Kidnapper." This will be an homage to the auteur method of filmmaking (Charlie Chaplin, Orson Welles, Jean-Luc Godard). If you think you can handle this breakout role, please show up to 16*** Ventura Blvd., Encino, California— across the street from the Taco Bell—for an in-person camera test.*

The eager actress in me thought, *I can act the shit out of this part!!*

The intuitive wise woman in me thought, *Huh—this seems weird.* (In no way should this cinematic masterpiece be confused with the 2001 video with the same name. Hey, a good title is a good title, but this was a completely different writer, director, producer, and story, not to mention many years earlier.)

I showed the letter to my cousin Benny Medina who was already in the entertainment business. At the time, he was an actor and singer, and years later would become a big manager. (Yes, *that* Benny Medina.) He said he would go with me as protection. I think he secretly wanted to kick this guy's ass if he was at all questionable.

At first it seemed like I should check it out. But upon further reflection, it really felt just too creepy and a waste of time and energy, so I didn't end up pursuing this little masterpiece. I was anxious to work, but I wasn't stupid.

Largely unbeknownst to me, "auditions" like this were happening all the time in those days. This was the world in which I, a budding young actress, had to use my scruples and my common sense to decline the offer to screen-test for a low-budget, auteur-esque, independent feature entitled *One of Our Cheerleaders Is Missing*.

I can only imagine what would or could have happened had I shown up, ready and willing to be tied to a wall while my demented writer/director/editor/actor made an art film with me. Yikes.

Then there was a casting I went on for a silly part as a teenager in some C movie, a wannabe slasher film disguised as a female-bonding narrative—give me a break. Regardless, I figured it was good to get in front of casting directors to show them what I could do.

The guy in the fluorescent-lit office with water-warped ceilings and moldy carpet really thought I was great. He was wondering if I would be interested in another film he was casting. He said the magic words: "The lead." Saying "the lead" to a young, hungry actress is like flaunting a juicy steak in front of a starving carnivore.

"Sure, I'd love to read it!"

He left the office and came back with a camera and some new sides ("sides" are basically a scene or two from the project stapled together). He said he would give me a few minutes to look it over and to let him know when I was ready.

In the scene, my character is being pursued by some guy at a Halloween party. She ends up going down to the basement, where she turns around and sees two guys standing there. For some reason (maybe she's drunk?) she says, "It's so hot in here," and takes off her top. She then starts to make out with one of the boys, while the other one tries to take his shirt off, but stumbles (he must be drunk too) and passes out.

Clearly, a comedy classic!

I think he was hoping that I was a method actor

and would actually remove my top. When I didn't, he suggested I drive with him to go meet the director at his house. I politely declined and left the building.

I didn't really think about it much—just another incident to avoid while pretending it wasn't weird so as not to alienate the casting director, in case he was casting a part I wanted in the future.

Maybe it was time to get an agent.

I used to sometimes joke how no one ever tried to hit on me; I'd never had a casting-couch moment—what was I, chopped liver? But looking back, I realize I did have several of these encounters. It's just that I was already so used to dodging the proverbial bullets, or ignoring them, or simply putting them in the category of "men and situations that must be avoided or expertly slipped away from," while causing the fewest ripples in the shark-infested waters of the world.

Vampire King

At some point my girl gang turned against me. Even Lexi, who I thought had my back no matter what, caved in to the mob mentality and betrayed our friendship. Teenage girls are the *worst*. Hormonal. They just can't help themselves.

I remember one time when I was working on *Killer Joe* with the late, great director Billy Friedkin. He had made one of my all-time favorite movies, *The Exorcist*. At the time, I was basically a stepmother to a very distraught and difficult teenage girl. I told Billy in a conspiratorial way, "I know what *The Exorcist* is really about . . . a fifteen-year-old, hormonal girl. Brilliant . . ."

He looked at me and said, "No. It's about a girl who gets possessed by the devil."

Same thing.

Anyhow.

My girl gang was pissed—and threatened—because I had started hanging out with some older kids. They didn't approve because they couldn't beckon me at their will. Girls can get really cunty and controlling at this age if they can't dominate you at all times. They would show their disapproval in passive-aggressive ways, like not speaking to me, or not letting me know that everyone was wearing purple one day, shit like that. I didn't deserve this sinister treatment, and much to their disappointment, I didn't take the bait. Their catty behavior definitely diminished the trust and respect I had for them, and for our bestie status.

I wanted to be friends with who I wanted to be friends with. The older kids were cool and smart. They knew stuff I didn't. So when I didn't bend the knee and kiss my gang's friendship bracelets, they iced me out. They wanted to break me. To have me come crawling back, begging for forgiveness and pledging eternal loyalty.

Suddenly they seemed super lame to me. A waste of energy. Making me feel somewhat smaller. Anxious. I'd find myself ditching school and hitchhiking to my happy place, the beach. Stupidly, I'd journey alone, thumb out waiting for a ride, through Topanga Canyon, then down to Dog Beach in Malibu. I'd get stoned and devour a pint of Häagen-Dazs carob ice cream while slathering my body with baby oil, and watch the cute surfer boys for hours. I deemed myself a surfer girl (I wore my puka shell necklace every day to prove it), even though my feet never touched a board. Luckily, I didn't encounter any shady behavior from the drivers. I made a point of sussing them out pretty hard before I'd enter their vehicle, but still . . . I was becoming more and more isolated from my supposed best friends, and I didn't actually hang with the older kids that much, it was more just saying hi when I saw them around school. So I was basically on my own. And that led me to depression. It was very clear: there had to be somewhere else in the world that would be better than where I was.

I was really into vampires then. I watched *Dark Shadows* religiously. Barnabas Collins was a two-hundred-year-old vampire who was cursed by this witch named Angelique after he rejected her love. He wanted to be a good guy, but struggled with his murderous vampiric impulses. Jonathan Frid, who played Barnabas, was just fantastic in it. Campy and intense all at the same time. Nothing was sexier to me than the idea of some vampire king coming to me in the middle of the night, taking me away, making me immortal, and loving me forever. I would pray in my canopy bed before I'd go to sleep for the Dark Lord to please come take me away.

When I explained to my mother how unhappy I was, that I knew there was another place that would be better for me, and that if I killed myself to please not take it personally, she stared at me, didn't say a word, and walked out of the room.

Later that night, my mom and dad both came into my bedroom and simply announced, "We're moving."

I was lucky to have parents who recognized that they had to get me out of this cesspool known as the Valley. It would have probably been worth a trip to a psychiatrist's office, or at least a discussion about what was up with me, but those were different times. Before such things like emotions and problems were talked about. At least in my household. Antidepressants might as well have been for the criminally insane, and ADHD hadn't even entered the cultural lexicon. My father didn't believe in therapy.

God bless my parents for doing the next best thing: they packed up our house and we moved to Beverly. Even though I protested, I was secretly excited for a new adventure over the hill.

PART II
Schooling

Each friend represents a world in us, a world possibly not born until they arrive, and it is only by this meeting that a new world is born.
—Anaïs Nin

One is not born, but rather becomes, a woman.
—Simone de Beauvoir

Playboy Mansion

My parents offered me three choices of schools: Buckley, a private school that was very regimented, with a strict dress code, which did not appeal to me for obvious reasons—who wants to be told what you can and cannot wear? Next was Westlake, an all-girls school, which was like, *No boys, no way.* Then there was Beverly Hills High School, which was known to have a great theater and dance department, but sounded too snobby, so I protested this option as well. I was in full surfer mode at that point and suggested Calabasas High or something near the beach.

But because my mother was an interior decorator with lots of jobs in Beverly Hills, and because my siblings had already moved out, and because my dad was traveling a lot, they decided we were moving to Beverly Hills. To be more exact, they decided we were moving to the *slums* of Beverly Hills. Meaning, not the high-end area—the elegant houses with beautiful swimming pools, or the fabulous estates once inhabited by the heads of studios and movie stars—but the more humble part of town with little duplexes, east of Doheny and just above Wilshire Boulevard. Beverly

High is technically a public school, but you have to live in Beverly Hills in order to attend it. We just eked into the zip code. My father's fabulous sister, Aunt Bobbie, also lived there, along with Uncle Jack and my three cousins. So I would in fact have some family nearby, which would be nice.

During my final few weeks of junior high at Parkman in the Valley, everyone kept telling me about this girl named Maggie who looked exactly like me and had just moved to the area and enrolled in our school for the final months of the term. Of course, I wanted to check her out, as anyone with narcissistic tendencies would want to do.

When I finally approached her, she turned around and we both looked each other up and down. Yep: same hair, same boobs, same waist, same hips, same height, same weight, same color eyes, same style. Needless to say, I liked her immediately. She was actually very beautiful—much prettier than me by a long shot—she had a bit of an Ali MacGraw vibe, with a low, husky voice. We both acknowledged that we did in fact look similar, if you blurred your vision, and a friendship was born.

I told Maggie that my family was relocating to Beverly Hills at the beginning of summer, and how I was *so* not into this move. Beverly Hills seemed, at that time, kind of like a gross place to me—full of rich, entitled people who I had nothing in common with. Maggie told me her family was renting a house in Malibu for the summer. She said I should just move in with them and that we could hang out on the beach for a month or two. Malibu!! Now we were talking! This, obviously, sounded like a great idea.

Maggie had a certain sophistication about her. She came from an artistic family who lived in the Fairfax district—she wanted to be a costume designer and her sister was involved in the movie business somehow. More importantly, she had an adventurous spirit that I really connected with. I did in fact move to Malibu to hang with Maggie, but only for two weeks; I needed to help my mom get our new place together before school started.

One afternoon, Maggie confessed to me that she had been hanging out at the mansion, swimming, watching movies, meeting cool people.

"Wait. You went to a *mansion*?"

"Yeah, I went to Hef's—every Friday night he has movies. It's so cool."

"What's a Hef?" I asked.

"Hef, as in Hugh Hefner," she explained, in a nonchalant, breezy way. "As in the Playboy Mansion."

I knew what *Playboy* magazine was—I did, after all, have an older brother. In fact, my mother had cleverly made one of the walls in my brother's bathroom a collage of *Playboy* magazine covers, centerfolds, and iconic sex symbols: Raquel Welch, Brigitte Bardot, Sophia Loren, etc. This was my introduction to the beauties of the sixties and seventies. My mom was cool like that.

So this whole idea of *Playboy* intrigued me. Maggie said that on Friday nights, Hef would invite all sorts of people over—actors, sports figures, the Playmates, and other interesting characters who happened to be around and wanted to watch a movie. He had a screening room and would play a popular new film. They'd have a huge buffet of food, a pinball arcade, a "grotto" (whatever that was), and a mini zoo. It sounded so fun. Let's be honest, she had me at free food and pinball arcade.

"I totally wanna go!"

Maggie explained that you had to be invited, that there was a "list." This was my first introduction to the concept of a guest list. She also mentioned that she would sometimes go there just to have a swim and play tennis on days when there wasn't a party. Some rich guy she knew with a Rolls-Royce Corniche, butter-yellow to be accurate, would drive her there.

"I'm really good at tennis," I chirped. "I've been playing since I was eleven!"

"Maybe I could ask about bringing you on a Saturday afternoon first."

"Whatever! It sounds rad."

The following week, Maggie called: "I have great news—Hef is having a costume party this Saturday and I got you on the list. It'll be really fun. We can dress up."

"Oh wow," I said. "What should we wear?"

The obvious thing, because we looked so much alike, was that we could dress up as twins. These were the days when you and your bestie would confer and often coordinate your party outfits, subtly sending out the message that you were a team.

We ended up wearing matching tight Winnie-the-Pooh crop tops, Chemin de Fer high-waisted jeans, red lipstick, and sneakers, and put our hair in pigtails. Despite our newly sprouted boobs, we still had an innocence about us. At least *I* did.

That Saturday night, Steve—aka Yellow Corniche Guy—picked us up at Maggie's place in Malibu and drove us over to Holmby Hills. There was a line of cars waiting to be parked in the famous circular driveway, and I sat there gawking at the biggest house I'd ever seen. It was like arriving at Disneyland.

The vibe was good. I remember seeing James Caan standing among several other actors I knew from the movies, as well as a few Playmates I recognized from my brother's bathroom. But most impressively, and hardest to miss, was Wilt Chamberlain.

My dad was a big Lakers fan and had floor seats since they started playing at the Forum in 1967. (He had even played basketball at UCLA for a bit.) So I grew up watching these incredible OG players: Wilt Chamberlain, Jerry West, Gail Goodrich, Elgin Baylor, Happy Hairston, Pat Riley. It was a thrill, yet a bit terrifying, to see these massive men sprinting toward me as they passed the ball back and forth. I loved going, and I loved seeing my dad yell at the top of his lungs—yes, he was one of those guys. On the way home, we'd stop at the iconic Randy's Donuts. It was great bonding time for my dad and me.

When I saw Wilt Chamberlain, I couldn't believe my eyes. I went right up to him and gushed about how I'd been watching him since I was six years old, how my dad had floor seats, all of this. He was very nice, though I had to crank my head back really far to talk to him because I only came up to his belly button. I was so excited to tell my dad.

Next, I went to check out the food. There was the huge buffet Maggie had mentioned—but more importantly, there was a whole display of desserts: brownies, cookies, cakes, pastries—a sugar junkie's version of heaven. I grabbed a stash and wandered into another room where there were all these pinball machines. I was like, *What!?* and immediately started playing. I couldn't believe no one else was in this fabulous arcade.

A guy came in and started talking to me, and I mentioned that it was my first time there.

"Would you like me to show you around?" he asked.

"Totally!" I was my mother's daughter after all, and needed to see what the joint looked like.

First he showed me the red room—impressive! The blue room—ooo! And lastly, he said, "Do you want to check out the grotto?" His tone made it sound like some secret, mysterious place.

Of course I wanted to see the grotto! What the fuck is a grotto?

The grotto, it turned out, was an indoor cave that flowed into the outdoor pool, and somewhere within bubbled a Jacuzzi. There were a couple of girls swimming around, and I couldn't see for sure but it looked like they were nude. I tried to act like this was the most normal thing in the world. My tour guide said, "Do you want to go in?" There was a sleazy glint in his eye, and I slowly realized that he was hitting on me.

I laughed and blurted out, "You know I'm fifteen years old, right?"

He started laughing too, and said, "You're funny. What are you, twenty-three? Twenty-four?"

"No, really, dude, I'm only fifteen," I giggled. "You could get in a lot of trouble."

When he realized I was telling the truth, his whole demeanor changed. He and his frozen smile backed away from me, then turned around and left me alone there in the infamous grotto.

I couldn't wait to tell my mom about the mansion. She was excited because she wanted to know what the interiors looked like. I told her about the molding, the wood, the peacocks, the famous actors. I obviously left out a few details.

The following Friday, when I was invited back to the mansion, I nonchalantly said, "I'm going to Hef's—it's movie night."

"No you're not," my mom declared. End of discussion.

I didn't return until a few years later, when my Uncle Jack was having a fundraiser for the Big O, the orchestra he cofounded, which was initially known as the New American Orchestra and later renamed the American Jazz Philharmonic. It consisted of more than ninety of the best studio musicians around and often debuted new works by young composers. My uncle was cool like that. In the sixties, Judy Garland saw him playing piano in a jazz trio in Paris, where he was living with Quincy Jones (oh, the stories I was never told), and brought him to California to be the arranger for her television show.

I remember the first time I went to Disneyland as a kid and took the "It's a Small World" boat ride. It was so magical and beautiful: global unity, different worlds, happy songs. But when I returned years later, the automatons were breaking down and the seats felt dirty—the seams were showing more than I'd recalled. That's kind of how I felt when I returned to the Playboy Mansion as an adult, for my uncle's fundraiser. Run-down, not so sophisticated, kind of sad and desperate.

It was around this time that I was out dancing one night at some LA nightclub with Jodie Foster, who I'd become friendly with at college. We had to be twenty-one to get into the club, but I guess since Jodie was famous, they let us in. Definitely a perk. As we were having fun, minding our own business, dancing away, some weird guy with a mustache approached me.

"Would you ever consider posing for *Playboy*? I know Hef, I could introduce you."

"Umm, no thanks."

"You'd be perfect. Just what they're looking for."

"No thank you. I want to be an actress so I don't think that would be a good idea."

"My wife, Dorothy, is an actress. And being the

centerfold totally helped her. She's now starring in a Peter Bogdanovich movie. Think about it." He handed me his business card and sauntered away. He was so slimy he practically left a trail of ooze in his wake. Jodie and I looked at the card, which had *Paul Snider* written on the front. Creepy. I threw it away and we got out of there.

Three weeks later, I read in the paper that Paul Snider had brutally murdered his wife—*Playboy* centerfold Dorothy Stratten. Then he'd killed himself.

In 1981, Bob Fosse, one of my favorite directors (please watch *All That Jazz* if you haven't already), made *Star 80*, a film about the tragedy. I was very happy not to have been a subject in that movie.

Hustling

My very first day at Beverly Hills High School, I showed up with feathered hair, white Dittos low-rider flare jeans, a super-tight powder-blue crop top, and a newly chipped front tooth. And, of course, I was wearing my talisman: my puka shell necklace that I had strung myself, full of Hawaiian power and protection, and, let's face it, looked oh so cool.

My first English class was like a Dr. Seuss book. There were three girls in a row, all with the same haircut, all with the same Louis Vuitton bag, and all with the same nose: a Dr. Diamond, I was told—the plastic surgeon who always left his signature mark on the side of his subject's nostril.

Then came Nutrition between second and third periods—"mods," as they called them. Sounded hipper. More progressive perhaps. There were even beanbag chairs and an outdoor smoking section. So I went to the cafeteria during Nutrition, and was immediately stunned. Not only was there pizza—*proper* pizza—piping hot from a pizza oven, and a really nice chef's salad, they also had Winchell's donuts (chocolate and glazed). Winchell's were the Krispy Kremes of that time. Super psyched, I succumbed to a chocolate donut and sat myself down in the shiny white dining hall.

It was like I was fresh blood in the water. Within minutes, some guy showed up, asked if I was new here, and shoved a glossy invitation in my face to his Uncle Fig's *Star Wars* party. I was used to "Hey, we have kegs, come by Friday," so I was pretty impressed with this slick-looking announcement. Turns out "Uncle Fig" was an older man who would drive around in a purple Excalibur and invite young girls to his parties. I guess his "nephew" must have been on the payroll.

Five minutes later, a second guy showed up, a big fellow. Asked if I was new. Introduced himself as Rob, captain of the football team. Quarterback. His way of welcoming me to Beverly Hills High School? "You wanna do some blow?"

"Sure," I casually replied. My mom did encourage me to make new friends. And I didn't want to seem rude. I just had to make sure I wasn't caught.

Beverly High was looking better by the second. Better food. Better drugs. Fancier invites. So the captain and I headed downstairs to the indoor parking lot.

The *indoor* parking lot? Yes. At Beverly High we had both indoor *and* outdoor lots. Naturally, the indoor one had all sorts of expensive cars. Mercedes-Benzes, BMWs, Corvettes, Porsches, Alfa Romeos. An impressive display of hand-me-down family mobiles and extravagant sweet-sixteen trophies.

Just moments after we slid into the quarterback's

El Camino and he pulled out some coke, there was an aggressive knock on the window. A security guard was glaring at us. *Shit*. Of course they had a security guard at Beverly High, what was I thinking? I was petrified. If I got busted on my first day, my parents would kill me.

I opened the passenger-side door and the guard asked for my name. Thank god my acting chops kicked in and I played the surefire card.

"Excuse me, I have to go!" I mustered up a perfect mix of horror, hysteria, and shame. "I just got my period and I left my purse in the car." It didn't hurt that I was wearing my new white pants. "I really need to get to the bathroom, like *now*. Thank you so much!" I slipped past the sentinel and scurried back toward the stairway to the school entrance, right after he wrote down my name.

By my fifth day at Beverly, I'd discovered a guy who sold quaaludes. We, too, became fast friends. Quaaludes—they were excellent. They gave you a tingly, numb, drunk feeling without the booze. (I wonder why they don't make them anymore!) The following week, between second and third mods—officially now known as Donut Time—Quaalude Guy introduced me to a dude named Justin.

Justin had a mop of thick brown hair that he kept flicking out of his face, and wore a crisp polo shirt and jeans that were way too tight for his doughy, nonathletic body. He was also sporting a pair of ugly brown Top-Siders sans socks, a pretentious look at any age.

Justin fondled a pair of dice over a pricey-looking backgammon board, and clearly thought he was the shit.

I greeted him and said, "Oh, wow, you play backgammon?"

"Yes, but I only play for money," he replied in a condescending rich-boy tone. I immediately wanted to take him down and make him smell his shoes.

I started messing around with my feathered hair, giving off insecure vibes, leading Justin to believe I was a total novice, a lamb waiting to be slaughtered. I made him feel like he was in control, like he was *the man*. He was probably one of those wealthy kids whose parents were never at home—the sort of guy who got everything he wanted except the attention and love he so clearly craved. Cliché, I know, but I witnessed a lot of that at Beverly.

"I've only played a couple times," I said nervously. "Does it have to be for money?"

"Actually," he leaned back in his chair like some gangster in a B movie, "since my regular didn't show up, I can lower my rates and make it a buck a chip. Lower than that isn't really worth my time."

"Well . . ." I glanced downward, darting my eyes back and forth (I had read somewhere that this conveys uncertainty). I bit my lower lip for that extra-special touch—another cliché, but effective. "Okay, I guess."

I sat myself down and proceeded to take this fucker's money. Every day, I'd end up winning about sixty bucks from Justin during the break between mods two and three. Every day, I'd sit down and beat this guy who had cash to spare and would shamelessly take less fortunates' lunch money without batting an eye. Every day, I would simply shrug and smile as he said how lucky I was and laid down more bills—determined to beat this new girl. I think I let him win a couple games, just to keep him on the hook.

As the hustle went on and I got more comfortable with the whole charade, I'd pop a quaalude to make it even more fun, then sit down with my chocolate donut and rake in my daily backgammon collection.

I was really loving this new school.

Then one day, during yet another game with Justin, some kid dressed in a Young Republican outfit—chinos, white shirt, and stupid loafers (I guess I have a thing against loafers)—came over and handed me a note: *The vice principal would like to see you in her office.*

I didn't recall booking an appointment with the authorities . . .

"Come. Now," the boy said, and waited for me to collect my things and follow him to Oz.

Did I mention I'd just taken another quaalude? Shit, fuck, fuckety shit, I could *not* get busted for whatever it was I was being persecuted for. I started going through a list of possible transgressions. It'd only been a few weeks. Nothing really came to mind.

My fingers began tingling and my lips went numb as I floated toward the office. I kept repeating to myself the Valley stoner's mantra: *Maintain. Maintain.* I felt my legs dissolving under my torso with each step. By the time I sat down in front of the vice principal—a stern lady in her sixties—I was in full-blown 'lude mode.

Vice principal: "So, I understand you were off campus in the underground parking lot during school hours? You know that is not allowed."

Ohhh, the *delayed* bust.

Once again, I went into one of my great high school performances, the words tumbling out of my mouth: "Oh my god, that was my very first day at school! I was so scared coming from the Valley and not knowing anyone here that I wore my favorite pants. They were white, and all of a sudden I got my period! I was so mortified, I had to walk with my hands behind my seat so no one would see the blood seeping through." I was beginning to cry and show signs of hysteria. "I'd left my purse in my new friend's car—"

"Okay, okay, calm down," the concerned old lady cut me off, handing me a Kleenex from a flowery box on her desk. She was extremely nice.

By the time I left her office, she had a protective arm around my numb and tingly shoulders, telling me that if I ever needed to talk to anyone, she was there for me. Bless her buttons.

I walked down the hall toward my astronomy class (in an actual planetarium) and gave myself a high five.

Beyond making money, getting better drugs, and going to the beach to surf as my PE elective, I was way more inspired by my new school than I had been by Parkman. (Mom, Dad, thank you—one of the best decisions you ever made for me.)

At Beverly, I met a group of like-minded people who were singers, dancers, actors, writers, and directors. There was a whole other side of the high school—a slew of young, exciting, driven artists. More than a few of them went on to become professionals in their chosen fields, and even in high school they offered me something to aspire to other than making a few bucks over pinball or backgammon.

One afternoon I met this kid in the cafeteria who went by the name "Romeo Blue." He was singing and playing a guitar. We quickly struck a bond and soon started sneaking into the school's little theater—he'd play drums or guitar and I would sing. At one point we ended up in a pit chorus together. We told each other that when we got older, we'd both make it to the big stage.

Romeo Blue, it turned out, was his stage name—his real name was Lenny Kravitz, and we've been friends ever since.

Aunt Bobbie had been great friends for many years, since she was around fifteen, with the parents of a few of my soon-to-be best friends: Jill, Roxanne, Morleigh, and Daryl. The girls, like their gorgeous mamas, were fun, sophisticated, and a bit intimidating at first. I was excited when they invited me to a dinner party at Roxanne and Morleigh's house. I got dressed up in my finest—a midnight-blue Capezio dancing outfit. When I entered their super-cool modern home that their very talented, groovy mother Lenny had designed, they were all there sipping exotic cocktails and looking chic in Kenzo, Sonia Rykiel, Emmanuelle Khanh, and other designers I had never heard of—not to mention elegant vintage dresses from the 1930s. There were about eight girls in all. *Whoa, Toto, I have a feeling we're not in the Valley anymore.*

Another girl named Tina Landau coined them the "Young Sophisticates." They introduced me to modern dance. Before long we were choreographing avant-garde pieces to the likes of Devo and performing them at school. Over the ensuing years, Morleigh and Roxanne danced and choreographed pieces all around the world, separately and together, and still do to this day.

Tina, perhaps the most talented person my age I'd ever met, also became one of my best friends. We'd play the piano and make up songs together outside of our musical-comedy class. I can spot a genius a mile away, and Tina was definitely that. She would eventually write and direct the first professional play I was cast in, and would influence me in so many ways. Like my dinner-party-dance girls, we remain great friends to this very day. I was beginning to find my tribe.

I tell you all this because I don't want to give the impression that all I did was hustle games for money. I started shedding my delinquent Valley ways and exploring more artistic endeavors. I was surrounded by creative people and many more opportunities for fun. Looking back, the only time I went into hustle mode was when I felt I was being disrespected or not taken seriously. That just because I was female, some guy felt like he automatically had the upper hand.

In 2006, I went to the premiere of *The Beatles LOVE* by Cirque du Soleil at the Mirage in Las Vegas. Since this was the opening, I had to dress up. I wore a long, beautiful, low-cut Etro dress. And since I am my grandmother's granddaughter, I had to go play poker. Texas Hold'em was a-callin'.

The casino was bustling. Unfortunately for me, all the lower-stakes tables were completely booked. The only seat available was at a no-limit, big-blinds table. Fifty-dollar small blinds, hundred-dollar big blinds. For those of you who don't play poker, just know that I usually play the tables with a five- or ten-dollar minimum bet—twenty-five- to fifty-dollar blinds if I'm drunk and feeling delusional. I only had an hour to play before meeting up with my friends, so I sat down at the big-blinds table with a bunch of loud men from Texas.

"Oh, look at the pretty little lady who's joined us!" the second-largest man said, eyeballing me from the neck down. "This is a big-boy table, girlie. You know how to play poker?"

"I've played a few times with my brother and his friends. It was fun!"

"Maybe you should go try the slots. I'd hate to take such a pretty lady's money." Condescension oozed from his cigar-smoking mouth as my stomach started to tighten.

"No, I think I'd like to play just a few games, if that's alright. I have to meet my boyfriend soon." (It's always good to mention a boyfriend in situations like this, even if he's imaginary.)

"Okaaay. Well, don't cry when we strip you dry and say you weren't warned."

I smiled demurely, playing into their idea of a vulnerable damsel. Hustle-mode kicking in, I bought some chips and sat my little-lady ass down.

I kept asking them all sorts of beginner questions—"Do we ante?" "What's the *river* again?" "Is this bet okay?"—and lost the first few hands. I wasn't necessarily losing on purpose, I had shit cards, but it gave me credibility as a complete novice.

Then, on about the fifth hand, I was dealt an ace of hearts and a jack of hearts, known as the "hole cards" which only you can see. Next came the flop (the community cards): eight of spades, king of hearts, queen of hearts. Another round of betting. Then, on the turn, came one more community card. A ten of clubs. More betting. Then the final community card, a ten of hearts.

Oh. My. God.

If you've never played poker, a *flush* is when you have five cards of the same suit. If they happen to be in consecutive order, that's known as a *straight flush*. Better yet, if you happen to pull an ace-king-queen-jack-ten, all in the same suit, you have a *royal flush*. It's the best possible hand, the crème de la crème. The mac daddy. It is unbeatable. I was trying my best to keep my facial muscles from moving and my breathing steady: the classic poker face.

If I was going for the long hustle, I would've dumped this hand. It was too soon to go in for the kill. But I was ready to leave—these guys were making me sick. I limped along, betting just enough to stay in the game. When someone else would raise the bet, I'd squirm a bit, which can be a "tell." The pot kept getting bigger and bigger. Most of the other players folded. But the guy in the cliché ten-gallon hat must have been sitting on two or three kings—a full house, perhaps? Four of a kind, maybe? Whatever he had, he clearly assumed he was the winner. Some other guy who also must have had a very good hand, perhaps three queens or tens, continued raising. I was running out of chips—there was a lot of money on the table at this point.

When it was my turn to bet again, I glanced at my imaginary watch to indicate that my time was running out and that I would have to go soon. "Well, I don't have that much left. Um . . . what if I just go all in?"

No response.

"Is that okay . . . ?" I asked.

"Are you sure you want to do that?" said the ten-gallon-hat guy.

"Yeah, I guess . . . Why not?"

The man twirled his cigar, kept staring at me, and after a beat matched my bet. I suddenly felt like I was in some old-timey Western and I was praying this guy wasn't packing. He smugly laid down his cards, confident that his kings-over-tens full house was a winner.

When I revealed my gorgeous royal flush, the table went dead quiet. The bells of the nearby slot machines seemed to be mocking the guy.

In an icy and threatening voice, Ten-Gallon Hat said, "Oh look, boys—I think we have a hustler on our hands." I tried not to laugh. Truth be told, anxiety was slithering through my body like a testy snake. My blood went cold. They all looked at me like they wanted to fucking gut me. I picked up my money, gave a nice tip to the dealer for gifting me such an epic hand, and graciously thanked the players.

"You can't just walk away with our money!" one of them snapped.

"Oh, I'm sorry. I wish I could stay but I have to go find my friends."

If looks could kill . . .

I must admit, the whole thing was really fucking satisfying—the same sort of delightful gratification I got from snatching Justin's daddy's dough back in high school.

I loved taking money from these guys who thought I was dumb because I had tits. The only way to shut them up was to look each of them straight in the eye, smile, scoop up the loot, and politely say toodle-oo. Manners matter.

Does this make me a cunt? I don't think so.

It was definitely an AlphaPussy move. Sometimes one must become the AlphaPussy in order to be the victor, not the victim. And maybe the next time those guys encountered a woman in a pretty dress, they wouldn't underestimate her.

The Magic People

Beauty and the Beast was the first play I ever saw. I'm guessing that I was around four. My mother took me on a Saturday afternoon to what seemed to be an enormous amphitheater. I was mesmerized. The lighting was dramatic. The energy was palpable. I thought the actors onstage were magical beings from another planet. (I even referred to them as "the magic people.")

When I first got to Parkman in seventh grade, I was confused when I went to the school play and saw classmates acting on the stage. These were not magic people! And not only that, they weren't even very convincing. I knew I could do a better job than them, and was compelled to start trying. So I took a drama class, started auditioning for plays, and before long got cast in the leads: Melody in *Melody Jones* and Rosie in *Bye Bye Birdie* (even though I auditioned to play Conrad Birdie; I was really into Elvis Presley and didn't see why a girl couldn't play a guy. It was called *acting*, for fuck's sake, but Mr. Ort, my first drama teacher and director of the play, kept saying to me, "But Rosie is the *lead*!"). Acting in these plays really sparked my interest. I had an instinct for it and thought it was really fun, but it wasn't until I got to Beverly High—surrounded by professional and semi-professional actors, parents who were in the business, and classes that were taken very seriously—that I decided this was what I was going to do with my life.

At Beverly, I could take musical theater with the legendary John Ingle, though in order to actually be in a musical, you had to audition. These auditions were tough. Some of the toughest I have ever experienced. And your classmates were allowed to watch, so if you fucked up, it was completely humiliating.

There was also a singing class with Joel Pressman. I didn't know shit about musicals at the time, so when he asked us to bring a song, I chose Joni Mitchell's "Twisted," while other people sang songs from *The Wiz, Annie, A Chorus Line*, and *Company*. I didn't grow up with musical theater; I had an older brother and sister who were into rock and roll, so that's what I listened to. My selection was ambitious, but I nailed it.

In my poetry class, the other students brought in the work of Yeats, Cummings, and T. S. Eliot, while I came with David Bowie's "Rock 'n' Roll Suicide." Luckily, the eighty-year-old professor made it clear to my peers, who thought I was cheating, that good lyrics were indeed considered poetry. He gave me an A.

In my dramatic acting class there were a few hard hitters—Joie, Shawn, Jeanette. They totally blew me away and made me realize that this was truly a *craft*. I knew then that I better work hard at it. The competition was gnarly. The better I'd perform, the more respect I'd get from others—and respect was something I thirsted for.

Oh, to be respected. At home, I was lucky if my brother and sister allowed me to sit in the same room with them!

I longed to hear that deep silence of awe after I finished a scene. I wanted the kind of silence that's better than applause—when someone is so affected or moved that they can barely breathe. I've only experienced this a few times—it is beyond satisfying. Don't get me wrong, applause is wonderful—and when it's real and earned and they truly mean it, it's like a hit of pure delight. But that silence, that forgetting-to-breathe lack of sound, that intense frequency of recognition, is utterly golden.

Having peers around who inspired me made me work harder, and drove my desire to constantly improve. This dynamic really changed the trajectory of my life. I became focused and passionate.

Jeanette, who was a few years older than me and just so good and deep and believable with her work, had studied at the American Conservatory Theater over the summer. It was a program up in San Francisco that you had to audition for. If accepted, you took professional classes in acting, speech, clown work, and scene study. Jeanette told me all about it and said it was a game changer. Seeing as I wanted to be as good as her, I decided I too must go.

But there was one little problem: you had to be seventeen years old to be admitted. By the time summer started, I'd be just turning *sixteen*. I figured one year of difference was hardly a concern, so I lied on my application and forged my parents' signatures. I sent it off and started preparing my monologues: a piece from the novel *The Waves* by Virginia Woolf, one from the French adaptation of the play *Antigone* by Jean Anouilh, and a third from *Cat on a Hot Tin Roof*. A few weeks later, I caught a bus to my audition in some auditorium on Sunset Boulevard.

I got in! I was so excited and proud when I received my letter of acceptance. Now all I had to do was convince my parents to let me go live in San Francisco for the summer. And of course pay for the program.

It was a hard no from my mother: "You're only fifteen—you cannot live alone in a different city!"

So of course I turned to my guy—my father. I told him how important it was to me, that this was what I wanted to do with my life, that I'd be sixteen by then, and that they *had* to let me go. He listened to me plead my case and then very diplomatically said, "I trust you. As long as you find someone older, an adult to live with, I don't see why not." God bless him.

Through some family friends, I found a woman named Michelle who worked on costumes in San Francisco. Michelle was twenty-eight—ancient! She told me she would be happy to split her rent with me for the summer. My mother finally agreed, provided there was always an adult around.

As soon as I walked through the doors to my new home for the summer—my parents in tow, checking that everything was kosher—Michelle pulled me aside and told me she'd just gotten a gig in Hawaii and was leaving in a few days. "No problem," I whispered, "just don't tell my parents." And so began one of the most expansive summers of my life.

Months later, when I returned from the American Conservatory Theater, I had more confidence in my acting—not to mention a bit of technique to work with. I may not have been aware of it then—but I sure am now—just how important it was for me to be surrounded by like-minded, creative, serious peers. There was no more idle time playing pinball and avoiding trouble. I now surrounded myself with dancers, singers, actors, writers, designers, people who had talent, passion, and focus.

It was soon thereafter that I joined the cast of my best friend Tina Landau's *Faces on the Wall*. Tina has gone on to make quite a name for herself and create incredible theater. Anyone who knew her back then isn't surprised. She was crazy talented even in high school and was emboldening to me as a young actress.

During the run of Tina's show that was presented at the Coronet Theatre, I started getting offers from talent agents. They wanted to sign me and said they'd immediately put me on television; they thought I'd kill on a sitcom. Very flattering, but I wasn't sure what to do since I was really hoping to go to college. This sentiment was also reinforced by David Hammond, who not only taught at Juilliard and Yale, but also at the American Conservatory Theater. After seeing my final scene presented at the end-of-summer program, David had been very encouraging and supportive of me becoming a professional actress, and strongly advised that studying subjects other than acting would only enhance my work. I felt the same way and was particularly interested in psychology and philosophy. My dream was to become a serious actress, à la Jessica Lange in the movie *Frances*, who could also discuss Jung, Freud, Heidegger, Nietzsche, and existentialism with all the smart-talking intellectual types I enjoyed hanging around so much. I wanted a well-rounded education, and hated the idea of being one of those vapid performers with nothing to talk about outside of my chosen profession. And the idea of being stupid scared me.

Martin Landau (no relation to Tina) was my main acting teacher in those days. I was friendly with his daughter Susie and had successfully convinced him to let me take his professional scene study class. He was a great actor, one whom I had long admired. He was always so captivating, whether he was the quiet thug in *North by Northwest* or Mark Antony's general in *Cleopatra* or portraying Bela Lugosi in *Ed Wood*—he always created grounded, believable, interesting characters no matter how extreme the premise. He was an actor's actor, an incredible human, and a wonderful teacher.

Martin was also the first professional to really take me seriously. So when the decision regarding agents and TV versus going to college came about, I turned to him for some sage advice.

"Well, Gina, there are always two roads you can take to get you where you want to go," he said. "There's the freeway, which gets you there faster, or you can use the country roads, which may take longer but can be a much more interesting and beautiful ride."

After much deliberation, I decided to go to college, to take the so-called country road. Martin even wrote me a wonderful recommendation letter. I really wish I still had a copy of that.

College Daze

I was hoping to go to the same college as Tina, though I didn't exactly have the grades nor the means to get into Yale.

I wanted to be at a theater-based school, but also wanted to take other classes. After applying to several places—and getting turned down by a few of them—I landed on Emerson College in Boston. It was a three-hour train ride from there to Yale in New Haven, Connecticut, and once my first semester started, I visited all the time. Not only to hang out with Tina, but to see her productions, other people's productions, and to sneak into some of the classes there. To this day, I still bump into people who thought I lived on campus in Calhoun, one of Yale's residential colleges.

It wasn't that I didn't like Emerson. But from the very beginning, I was getting cast in the main stage shows that were usually reserved for juniors and seniors. Not that I was complaining, but I wasn't really learning very much in my acting courses. In hindsight, Emerson had excellent creative writing classes, and I wish I had taken more of those.

I ended up getting a part in a professional production of *Runaways* at the Charles Playhouse in Boston that ran for many months. After that experience, I decided I wanted to transfer to New York University—there were great acting teachers there, and it seemed a lot more serious than Emerson. I applied, auditioned, and was accepted.

At NYU, part of my curriculum would be studying in an established studio, and there were several good options, including Circle in the Square, Lee Strasberg, and Playwrights Horizons.

I'd heard about a teacher named Terry Hayden at Circle in the Square who was supposed to be phenomenal, and decided to audit one of her classes. Early in the semester, she was doing what was called an "animal exercise," where you "become" an animal and then, eventually, incorporate those qualities into a character you're playing. When Terry asked for volunteers and no one raised their hand, mine shot up. Of course I chose a cat. I skipped the first step—fully depicting the animal—and started walking around on two feet, with feline qualities fully integrated into my human character.

Terry was impressed and said I could immediately advance to the second year of the program—and thus, go straight into my sophomore year.

NYU wasn't nearly as expensive then as it is today, but it was still pricey. And even though I liked the idea of living in a dorm, that would add a lot to the costs, so I had to find my own, cheaper place to live.

I got lucky at first when a friend who was living at her nana's apartment at 8th Street and Fifth Avenue, close to some of my classes, said I could be her roommate for two hundred dollars a month. This was a real steal. But the following year when Nana returned, I was back to square one and needed to find a new home.

I took classes in existentialism, psychology, and literature, in addition to my three days of studio work at Circle in the Square, but perhaps my most practical education was learning how to find an affordable apartment in New York City. I did all the typical things—put up notes on the boards at school, checked out *Roommates Wanted* lists at various restaurants, and so on. I'd even look at obituaries—who died? Whose apartment was now available? A classic New York move.

One day, my friend Monique—a sweet girl, although a little scattered at times—told me she had found a really cool place with another actress friend and they needed two more roommates. The fourth girl who'd be part of our new living situation was a model I didn't know. There were four bedrooms, and even though it was on First Avenue and 57th Street—pretty far from all of my classes—we'd only be paying $250 a month each. The price was right, and I agreed to join them before even checking it out.

The building was pink and featured a baroque wooden staircase. When I first walked in, the living room felt almost like a performance space. There was a painted mural behind a couch, framed by draped curtains. I thought, *Wow, we can put on our own shows in here!*

I claimed the smallest room, which was isolated just off the kitchen. It was tiny, and there weren't any windows, but it was separated from the other girls and felt like its own space. Plus, I always liked to be near the food.

One day when I was alone in the apartment writing a paper on Dostoevsky's masterpiece *Crime and Punishment*, something very strange happened. I was at the typewriter in the living room in just my underwear and eating a bowl of Grape-Nuts. (For some reason, I didn't like to be encumbered by clothes when I typed.) I suddenly felt someone staring at me. I glanced around but I was indeed alone.

Yet the feeling persisted. It's hard to explain, but I could see—not exactly with my eyes, more like with my other senses—this big dumb guy just watching me. He was dirty, unshaven, and wearing soggy underwear. He was looking at me with a vacant, menacing expression on his face.

I said, to seemingly no one, "Hey! Go away! Fuck off! . . . I'm writing here! You need to go away!"

Okay, clearly I was hallucinating.

When this happened a second time, however, I told the other girls that we had a ghost in the house. They just laughed at me.

My boyfriend at the time would often stay over in my windowless room. Some nights I'd wake up in a panic, like I was being suffocated, and discover small scratches all over my body. When I confronted him the first time, he said he hadn't done anything. And I kept waking up with the same little scratches and slight bruises on my neck, even when he wasn't staying over.

I knew something was afoot, yet no one believed me.

Then one afternoon I was off at rehearsal and Monique called and asked if she and her boyfriend could use my room for some privacy. I obliged. Later, I returned home, and just as I opened the front door of the apartment, the two of them came running and screaming out of my bedroom. I thought there was a fire or something, and walked cautiously into my room. There was a light flashing on and off in my little closet, a closet that had absolutely no access to a light source. I knew it was the ghost.

"Fuck off! You've got to get out of here!" I was pissed; this ghost was really starting to annoy me.

Finally, my roommates started to take me seriously.

Several weeks later, I was in California and Monique called me completely freaking out: "Mae [the aforementioned model] put bleach in the orange juice! She's trying to kill me!"

"Put her on the phone," I said.

A few moments later, a lethargic voice came on the line: "Yeah?"

"Mae, what's going on??"

In a strange, slightly Southern voice, like a possessed Mary Tyrone on a bender, Mae whispered, "*I told her not to drink my orange juice.*"

"Why was there bleach in the orange juice, Mae?"

"I'm trying to dye my elbows."

Beat.

"Put Monique back on the phone."

"Hi."

"Monique, pack your things and get outta there," I said. "I think Mae might be possessed. Or she's just fucking crazy. We need to find a new place."

That was the sequence of events that led us to our next new apartment on the corner of Houston and Mott. We left the other girl, who had brought in Mae in the first place. Fuck her. She was pretty strange as well. Monique may have been meek, but she was mighty fast at finding apartments. And at least I trusted her not to murder me in the middle of the night.

Rent at this new place was relatively cheap, and we would each have our own bedroom. At the time, this area was known as the Bowery, chock-full of derelict buildings and unhoused people, quite gritty all around. I wanted to check it out, and the landlord told me that the only time he could show me the apartment was at midnight. Any day of the week, but it had to be midnight. Okayyyyyy.

This was obviously a red flag, but it was always so tough and competitive to find an affordable place to live, so I just said sure, no problem.

I remember getting a little stoned and going to see *The Seventh Seal* before that midnight meeting. I had never seen an Ingmar Bergman movie before and was completely blown away—I'd been transported into a super-weird, nihilistic place where beautiful blondes talked about faith, God, death, and meaning. I was in heaven. Maybe I should learn to speak Swedish?

By the time I got downtown to check out the apartment, it just seemed like an extension of that bizarre Bergman world. My potential new landlord called himself Mr. Pierre—he told me he spoke ten different languages, and repeatedly claimed that he'd made the East Village what it was. His accent was Eastern European–ish, with a hint of Brooklyn, perhaps. He also said he was a jiujitsu master who was capable of breaking anyone's neck at any given moment. He had long, greasy, comb-over hair and was wearing fake Porsche sunglasses and a cheap suit that was covered in dandruff. After our little meeting, he said he'd let us rent the apartment on a month-to-month basis.

At the end of every month, this peroxide-blond German fräulein in a tight, low-cut, frilly dress would come over to collect our rent in cash. Clearly something odd was happening, but I dug the place enough to just go along with it.

Mr. Pierre liked us just fine until the day my boyfriend moved in with us. The guy I was seeing had just gotten kicked out of his Hell's Kitchen apartment—we were both at NYU, directing and acting together, and it would make the rent cheaper. It was more of a practical than romantic decision.

Mr. Pierre did not like this setup. He began calling my mom every night, ranting, "I made the East Village what it is! Your daughter is so sweet, so kind, and she invites me to her shows. But then her boyfriend moves in, smokes pot, and he leaves his bicycle in the hallway! I'm a jiujitsu master—I will break his neck!"

Needless to say, this freaked my mother out.

The situation just kept getting worse. One of our windows broke and it was the dead of winter. Every time I called Mr. Pierre to talk about it, he would merely reiterate that he made the East Village what it was. He had a very limited repertoire.

My boyfriend started saying that we shouldn't pay him because cold air was blowing in, and brought up the idea of taking Mr. Pierre to court. I was so *not* into taking legal action, but I let my boyfriend and a lawyer talk me into it. We soon discovered that Mr. Pierre had about ten other aliases. Indeed, he was a true slumlord and was not a newcomer when it came to court appearances. Every time I glanced over at him during those proceedings, he would silently growl at me like a rabid dog and mouth, *I'm a jiujitsu master, I will break your neck!*

Ultimately, we won the case and the court declared that Mr. Pierre owed us $10,000. For a moment, I thought we were rich—until the lawyer took $6,500 of it. The court also ruled that if Mr. Pierre didn't compensate us within two weeks, we'd win the whole building as a settlement. He paid us in the nick of time. Soon thereafter, however, we got out of that place—it was a hostile environment.

This area, all cleaned up and trendy, is now being called "Nolita," short for "North of Little Italy." Soho is just to the west, and the Lower East Side only a couple blocks away. That building is worth a fortune today.

* * *

One evening, after a day spent looking for yet another apartment, I was out with a bunch of people and I asked if they knew about any affordable living situations. One of them inquired why I had to leave the place I was currently in, and about where I'd been living before.

When I said my previous place had been at First Avenue and 57th Street, one of the other guys in the group chimed in: "The pink house?"

"Yeah. Do you know it?"

"Dude, do you know the story behind that house?" he asked.

"No . . ."

This guy proceeded to tell me that at the dawn of the twentieth century, that pink house with its baroque wooden staircase had been a brothel. Evidently, it had been shut down because the madame's son was mentally unstable—he'd strangled two of the prostitutes to death.

That was my ghost.

Poor guy. Stuck in the past. Some people just don't know how to move on.

Fuck-You Money

My dad happily paid my tuition for Emerson College and then NYU, but told me that I had to make my own "fuck-you money."

Back then, if I wanted, let's say, a stereo, my dad would respond, "Sure—you pay for half, I'll pay the other half." But don't be mistaken, that's not fuck-you money.

His advice was this: "Always have enough money of your own that at any given time, you can tell someone who wants you to do something that you don't want to do, *Fuck you!* and walk away. Fuck-you money gives you freedom. I'll pay for your tuition and housing, but you should make your own fuck-you money."

Fair enough.

The summer before my sophomore year—when I'd be moving to New York City from Boston—I definitely needed to make some money. Waiting tables while I was studying acting might sound cliché, but it had its benefits: it was quick cash with untaxed tips and free food.

Despite being a terrible waitress, I still got great

tips. I learned pretty quickly that if I said it was my birthday when a customer asked how I was doing, that pretty much guaranteed a big tip. Tight T-shirts helped as well. I'm slightly ashamed to admit that *Big nips get big tips* was an inside joke with one of my chesty coworkers. I wasn't working at Hooters or anyplace like that. Just a regular café. Decent food. Nice people. And customers who would leave good tips if I was sassy and clever.

The money I made would cover food for the semester. In those days, when I could eat absolutely anything without worry, in the morning I would grab my very own breakfast of champions on the way to school: three donuts—one chocolate old-fashioned, one chocolate glazed, and one old-fashioned with glaze. At lunchtime, I'd go to Ray's Pizza for a buck a slice—cheap, filling, and delicious. And then, for some reason, at night whenever I was writing a paper, I'd munch on Grape-Nuts. I think the satisfying crunch helped me to stay focused.

Despite my thrifty food budget, I still needed fuck-you money. I ended up getting a gig at the very cool Cafe Central. Actors, musicians, directors, and producers often lined the tables. Bruce Willis was a bartender (my actor boyfriend didn't like him much—I think he was threatened by Bruce's charm and swagger), and Sheila Jaffe was a hostess (and later became a prominent casting director). One night I spotted Mickey Rourke from *Body Heat* dining there.

The owner of Cafe Central understood that I was in school and often doing shows that would conflict with my waitressing schedule. Unlike managers in my past, he was very understanding about it: "Don't worry, kid, do your show, then come back to work. Hope it goes great!"

In between semesters, when I'd go back to LA, I'd search for any work I could find. They would be quickie jobs, something I would only do for a few weeks or a few months, depending on the break, before heading back to school.

One job in particular that I read about in a want ad seemed like a no-brainer. Here was the deal: For eighty bucks a day, I would bring this guy a *New York Times* and a cappuccino at eight thirty a.m. Then, at five thirty p.m., I'd bring him a bottle of Coca-Cola (it had to be a bottle) and a quarter pound of fruit salad from Greenblatt's, a deli off Sunset Boulevard; no other fruit salad would do. He didn't specify where the paper, coffee, or Coca-Cola should come from. Lucky for me, Greenblatt's had it all—it was one-stop shopping.

After I made the five-thirty drop, my boss would sign off for the day, thanking me and giving me two air-kisses, followed by a "Love ya, baby."

This guy supposedly had the largest rock and roll collection in the world. His tiny house in the Hollywood Hills was completely covered—wall-to-wall, shag carpet to cottage cheese asbestos–filled ceilings, couch, side tables, kitchen countertops, every inch of every surface—in something rock and roll. He had backstage passes, tour stickers, band T-shirts, key chains, set lists, posters, and signed photographs of popular bands from the seventies and eighties. There was stuff from T. Rex, the Rolling Stones, Led Zeppelin, Rush, the Clash, Yes, Pink Floyd, Black Sabbath, and on and on. He was constantly selling or buying, hustling or schmoozing; his black frizzy hair was seemingly glued to his phone. The guy never left the house! And he always wore shaded glasses, even though his hovel was dark as a mole hole. Perhaps he was some kind of bookie, ticket scammer, or drug dealer? Whatever he was, he suddenly needed to leave town after only two weeks of my employment, so I had to find another gig.

I decided to try my hand at being a chauffeur—the ad asked what kind of car I drove, if I had an up-to-date license, and if I was an excellent driver. At the time, my mom was letting me drive her old Audi—a nice enough car. And sure, I told them, I was an excellent driver—been driving since I was fourteen. By the time I had gotten my license in high school, I'd already been the designated driver on Friday nights since I was capable of driving semi-wasted—it's how I learned. Once, I got stopped with booze, weed, and a quaalude in me. Yet by the time I pulled away, the cop was smiling and said, "Have a lovely night!" I said, "You too!"

I could really hold my own.

Now let me make this very clear . . . I am completely against driving under the influence—it's selfish, stupid, and it's not fair. That being said, a few years ago I found myself way too high on mushrooms to be driving on Sunset Boulevard. I had just gotten back from a diving trip in Papua New Guinea, where I thought it was so cute how little minnows would swim next to a huge whale in order to stay protected. So, when I saw a cop car pull up next to me, my usual fear—*Oh my god, oh my god, I need to get off this road!*—turned to my newfound wisdom of the sea. I thought, *Ohhh, the cop car is like the big whale. So if I swim next to it, I'll be protected from all the other wasted drivers out there.* I rolled down my window, said hello and happy new year to the cops, and told them I was scared of all the drunk drivers on the road. I asked if I could drive near them on my way home, like a little minnow. They were very sweet, obviously charmed, said happy new year right back, and obliged my request.

I thought that was pretty clever.

But seriously, it's not cool to drive wasted. Shame on me.

The chauffeur gig paid a hundred dollars for the day—I was in! My first morning on the job, I picked up some pleasant-enough guy who was a salesman of sorts in the clothing business. I was supposed to drive him downtown, to the land of schmattas and deals, wait for him, then drive him back to his hotel on Beverly Boulevard.

It was a disaster. In order to get downtown, I had to take the freeway. Did I mention I'm terrible with directions? I guess I forgot to mention that to him as well, and next thing I knew we were completely lost and late for his important meeting. These were the days before Google Maps.

I kept apologizing. He was a very nice guy, but clearly—and for very good reason—he was pissed. When we finally got to the meeting, I redeemed myself a bit by adding my two cents about his designs and suggested a few color blocks. That, I was good at. I drove him home and never heard from him again. And so ended my short-lived career as a limo driver. Next.

I figured I'd have to go back to waitressing. Not the most stimulating work, but in the time left on that school break, it would have to do.

I went up and down Sunset Boulevard, Melrose, and all over Beverly Hills, but no one was hiring. This was ridiculous—I couldn't get a waitress gig? Frustrated, I decided to walk into a place called LA Sushi on La Cienega, knowing that they probably wouldn't hire me. When the owner asked me if I was at all Japanese, I cheekily replied, "My grandmother had a little Japanese in her." Fortunately, the lame joke flew over his head. He kept staring at me—"You know how to speak any Japanese?"

I rambled off, "*Ichi, ni, san, shi, go, roku, shichi,*" then mumbled the rest. I really only knew how to count to seven. (Where I learned even that much, I could not tell you.)

He seemed pleased with my response: "We are starting a new thing called Sushi Girl from Tokyo. Can you look more Japanese?"

"Uh, sure!" (Always say yes! Hey, I'm an actor, I can look like anything!)

"Great, you're hired. Come tomorrow for training. Look Japanese."

Well, I really wasn't expecting that, though I was curious if I could actually pull this off. It could be a fun acting exercise, I thought. At the very least, I might learn how to make sushi. Yay, a gig!

The next day, I made myself up as Japanese as I could. I pulled my black hair back tight and added some fake hair so I could fashion a long braid. I made my face up so it looked like I had pale skin, with pink accents to my cheeks and just a dash of red in the center of my mouth so it appeared smaller and more demure. I added liner and shadow to give my eyes a more Asian vibe. I thought I looked pretty cool! But it would have to be my demeanor that would really sell it. Calm. Respectful.

When I arrived, I was the only white person there. The boss instructed about ten of us in how to prepare the sushi. When I was asked to try, he was horrified at my skills. I was like a Neanderthal.

"You don't grab the rice like that!" He deftly showed me—wet hands, pick up the rice, one-two slap, dab of wasabi, piece of fish. I tried, but clearly I was still disappointing him.

No matter. About a half hour later, he announced very proudly to all: "Tomorrow night: grand opening!"

Wait, *what*? "Oh, no, no," I pleaded, "I need more rehearsal!"

"Don't worry, you'll be fine. We will call you Mariko."

"Mariko? Why Mariko?"

"Nice, clean, organized girl."

Not exactly how I would describe myself, but sure, I was willing to play along.

Right away, customers wanted to buy me saki. In my most polite voice, I would decline. I definitely couldn't drink while I was working. That wouldn't be very professional.

My boss pulled me aside. "Customer buy you drink, you drink it."

I couldn't tell if I was breaking some Japanese etiquette by turning down a drink or if I was just preventing more sake sales. Either way, I started drinking.

After a week, my boss gave me some Japanese phrases to say. I wasn't exactly sure what they meant, but everyone would laugh when I said them—including me, giggling softly, hand over mouth. Only once did someone come in who recognized me behind my disguise.

"Gina??"

My eyes flashed him a *Don't blow my cover* look, and I very deliberately said, "No, I'm Mariko."

I didn't know the guy that well—I think I'd met him at a studio; he was most likely some junior executive. I had no idea what he was thinking, but it had to be along the lines of: *She is insane*. Or maybe he just thought I was some nutty actress preparing for a role. In those days, white people were allowed to play any ethnicity, gender, or age without getting into trouble.

Or maybe he wasn't thinking about me at all. We waste so much time considering what people are thinking about us, when they are just as likely to be wondering what floss works the best and if it's even as important as dentists say it is.

My boss, who had seen the exchange and always seemed a bit tipsy, patted me on the back and said, "It's a good thing you are an actress with a cute personality, because one day someone from 20th Century Fox will come in and put you in *People* magazine!"

After three weeks, as entertaining as this all was—and as good at making maki rolls as I had gotten—I'd barely earned any money. And I think I was becoming an alcoholic.

Sadly, it was time for me to retire Mariko and seek out a different job—one that really paid.

Chippendales

One night, my sister and I thought it would be funny to go check out the male strippers at Chippendales. It had been all the rage for over a year and we were curious.

Chippendales was a dance venue with hot men stripping for a bunch of screaming women—sounded like a fun ladies' night out, and some great bonding time for the Gershon women. Tracy and I convinced my mom we should all go together.

When I was growing up in Los Angeles, anyone under twenty-one years old who wanted to go to bars, dance in clubs, see live music, or buy booze needed a fake ID. It was like a rite of passage once you turned sixteen. According to my driver's license, I was a twenty-eight-year-old woman named Marilyn, with long, light-brown hair, a patrician nose, and green eyes. I paid fifty bucks to this kid at my school who was known as the fake-ID guy. Maybe this license was his big sister's, maybe it was his aunt's. I didn't know, didn't care, didn't ask.

The truth about fake IDs was that no one really looked at them too carefully. A cheap trick, one which

I'm not proud of, was always wearing a tight top when using my fake ID. My boobs made me look older. Who checks if your face matches your ID when there are boobs to look at instead?

More important than my chest, though, was how I sold it. For example: Once I went into a liquor store to buy a bottle of tequila and handed my ID to the guy behind the counter. He looked at the picture, looked at me, and said, "This isn't you."

Instead of panicking, I coolly stared him straight in the eye and told the truth: "It isn't. It's a fake ID I bought off this kid at school. I'm only sixteen." My eyes never wavered from his. This is key: Do not ever break eye contact. Exude confidence. Be polite.

After a few seconds, he averted his eyes, laughed like we were old friends, took my cash, and sold me the booze. The double-psyche-out—it worked every time.

Tracy, my mom, and I ventured off to Culver City to that small, skanky palace that promised a smutty good time. We were seated around the main stage, among the throngs of overly excited women, probably out of the house for the first time in years, the bass throbbing so loud you could feel it pound against your rib cage. A hot, mustachioed, shirtless waiter with a bow tie came to take our order. His name was Randy.

Oiled-up dancers grinded into screaming women's faces. Repressed, horny housewives—the kind who religiously read Danielle Steel novels—let their greedy, deprived hands fondle the dancers' tight tushies as they enthusiastically thrust dollar bills into the men's skintight, skimpy Speedos.

We ordered some shots, and then some more, and then some more—really getting into the Chippendales groove.

When Randy was handing us our bill as we were ready to stumble out, I commented that he must make a shitload every night.

"Oh yeah, I clean up," he said. "But the cocktail waitresses are the ones who really pull it in—about five to eight hundred dollars a night, easy."

This caught my attention. "*What* cocktail waitresses?"

"After the show is over, Chippendales turns into a dance club and we let in men, excited to meet all the juiced-up ladies. That's when the cocktail waitresses come in and take over. I'm telling you, they really rake it in for just working about four hours. And it's all in cash."

Five to eight hundred dollars in four hours? Cash?! And here I was waitressing at a place called Moustache Café, barely making seventy bucks per lunch. (I only stayed because I was obsessed with their chocolate soufflé. So fucking good.)

Before I knew it, the words "I wanna work here!" came sloshing out of my mouth.

"You're over twenty-one, right? You have an ID?" He knew.

"Yup. I got in here, didn't I?"

"Let me introduce you to the owner. You'd kill here."

And meet him I did.

"You twenty-one?"

"Yup."

"You have ID?"

"Yup."

"Great. You're hired. Come tomorrow to get your outfit and sign some paperwork."

I went back to tell my mom and sister and we just laughed and laughed.

The next morning, when my hangover woke me up, I wasn't laughing quite so hard.

Fuck. What did I do? I can't work at that skanky place!

It goes without saying that I had lied the night before and told the owner I'd been a cocktail waitress all over New York City—downtown, uptown, and everywhere in between. In truth, the closest I'd ever come to cocktail waitresses was never.

However.

It was my first year studying acting at NYU, and in one of my classes I was working on a scene from David Rabe's *In the Boom Boom Room*—with Bridget Fonda, of all people. I didn't really understand the life of a stripper and thought, if anything, I could at least work at Chippendales for one night just to grasp the vibe.

Unlike the night before, my mother now seemed to disapprove and told me I needed to ask my father. Of course he would say no. But when I told him about the job, how much money I could make, and why I wanted to do it, he once again said that it was my decision. Our deal was that if there was ever a moment I felt uncomfortable, I would leave. Just get up and walk out. He trusted me.

Steve Banerjee, owner and creator of Chippendales, told me the rules, the hours, and gave me the "uniform"—a black and green corset that I still have today. eBay anyone?

(Fun fact: The aforementioned Paul Snider—from the "Playboy Mansion" chapter—was the same guy who suggested to Banerjee that he add male strippers to his then-struggling nightclub. The bow tie–and–cuffs costume was a nod to the *Playboy* Bunnies' outfits. Ah, the web of degenerates, creating dreams and fantasies all over Los Angeles.)

I had to try on the uniform and show him. I pretended it wasn't sleazy, but it was. It covered me up as much as any leotard I would dance in, though I had really long hair then, which conveniently fell over my pushed-up cleavage.

I just kept thinking, *Ohhh, this will be good for my scene . . .*

If he tried to make a pass at me, I would do what I had always done before with gross men: pretend it didn't happen. I'd put up an invisible shield between my person and theirs, with a bravado that read as, *Don't fuck with me because I'm not interested, and making me say the words out loud will only be an insult to your fragile ego, so let's not pursue this any further and avoid all possible humiliation that will be even more damaging to your existing lack of self-esteem and manhood than a swift kick in the balls.*

It turned out that cocktail waitressing was easier than I'd thought. This older French waitress showed me how to hold the tray without dropping all the drinks, how to separate the singles, fives, tens, and twenties in my hand, and how to bend my knees and keep my back straight when setting the drinks down so my boobs wouldn't spill out.

I made around $850 that first night in four easy hours. I would be home for another three weeks and that sort of money could really add up, so I returned the next night. And the next. To avoid sexual overtures from customers and solicitations from the male dancers, I called myself Tarquin and pretended that I was gay and had a trigger-happy girlfriend who lived in San Diego. For the most part, it worked.

I also pretended that I was unaware of the private parties that a few of the blonder gals would be invited to by certain foreign customers. I declined every proposition, including first-class plane tickets to places like Paris, Japan, and Dubai that, on a few occasions, landed on my tip tray.

I also didn't hide my disdain and was pretty vocal about Tuesday nights—mud wrestling—when female "dancers," the headliners for the evening, would dress up in costumes (Bucking Bronco, Plantation Polly, Lil' Bo Peep, etc.) and then strip down to their bathing suits. Like the male strippers, they would go around and kiss those who were handing out dollar bills. Once the men were good and drunk, the highest bidder would be able to mud-wrestle one of the bikini-clad gals.

The girls almost always won, which was a relief—fighting off these guys trying to paw at their boobs or pin them down. If things got too close, too rowdy, or too touchy-feely, there were big bouncer boys around the stage to protect any damsel in distress.

One night, however, I was called into the office and told that Cindy (aka Bucking Bronco) was sick and not able to come in. "You need to take her place," one of the two managers said. "Her costume is backstage. You will go third; you'll get a hundred bucks up front and then keep any tips you make."

I was pretty cocky at this point since I knew I had quickly become one of their highest grossers. But I didn't like the presumption that I would automatically accept the role of Bucking Bronco. I stayed fairly calm, my dad's voice whispering in my ear: *If you're ever uncomfortable, just walk out.*

"Sure . . ." I replied. "But here's the deal: I will do the dance, but I will absolutely *not* kiss anyone, and instead of the hundred dollars up front, I want five hundred."

After a moment and a few chuckles, one of them said, "That's ridiculous. We can't give you five hundred up front, especially with no kissing."

I spun on my heels and headed for the door. At the threshold, I turned back and said, with Bette Davis bravado, "Don't ever bring this up to me again."

I soon returned to NYU and executed a pretty decent

version of the character Chrissy in the *Boom Boom Room* scene. However, I didn't want to go out with anyone for the next year. The idea of sex made me tired. It made me want to take a bath with lovely oils so I wouldn't recall the skanky, dank smell of that fucking club. Working there, around that constant circus of sleaze and transactionalism, obviously had a negative effect on me. Do I wish I hadn't worked there? Hard to say. It definitely gave me more tools to help maneuver scuzzy situations that I would encounter in the future.

Years later, in October 1994, Steve Banerjee would die of suicide a day before his trial for attempted arson, racketeering, and murder for hire. There would be several TV movies made about Steve and his rise and fall in the seedy world he created. Chippendales revues and clubs are still thriving all around the world today.

Direct Yourself

The best advice always seemed to point to making my own decisions. Even when I got offered a role in *Friday the 13th Part 2*, psyched as I was, I was concerned about the topless scene. At the time, those kinds of slasher movies always had girls dying with their breasts exposed. My character would be killed by a stake through the heart, blood dripping down her tits. That seemed pretty lame to me: Exploitation 101.

When I asked my dad what he thought, I was secretly hoping he would say something like, "There's no way you're doing this. No daughter of mine is going to be topless for all the world to see." Instead, he took a beat and simply said, "It's *your* body. If you're comfortable with it, I'm comfortable with it."

I turned down the part.

My dad may have died too soon, but he taught me many valuable lessons in the nineteen years I had with him. Mainly he taught me to trust myself in making my own decisions.

This theme of trusting my gut kept showing up in my

life. My last year at NYU, I was fortunate enough to be one of the people who future Pulitzer Prize–winning playwright David Mamet invited up to Vermont to study with him for the summer. He and actor/director William H. Macy would be teaching their acting method, based on Sanford Meisner's technique.

The experience was intense and informative. David was not the easiest guy to talk to; I was intimidated by him—by his brilliance and by his no-bullshit demeanor. He wasn't exactly a fun-loving guy, but I respected the hell out of him and always wanted to impress him with my work. At the end of summer, after my final scene for the workshop, he pulled me aside and told me that I had a great sense of play and that I wouldn't have any trouble getting work. I was surprised by this—it was the biggest compliment I could expect from him. He then said the only advice he could give me was to learn how to direct myself.

I didn't understand.

Without any irony or sarcasm, he explained that if I was lucky, I'd work with two or three good directors during my entire career.

I thought that was very cynical and told him so.

"And that's if you're lucky," he repeated. "Learn how to direct yourself."

As time ticked on and I began to get work, David's pessimistic viewpoint proved to be a sad reality. I have found that most of the time—with a few notable exceptions—directors give you no direction (which, it turns out, is favorable to *bad* direction). Every good actor has at one time or another been given the lamest direction in the world—the kind of that makes absolutely no sense, yet has to be heeded so as to appease the director's ego.

My strategy? Simply say, "Oh, yes, I got it," then do it the way it feels best to me. Nine times out of ten, the director will be pleased with the result and move on. If you are a working actor reading this, you know exactly what I'm talking about. I didn't make up this method. All you can do is be responsible for your character and keep hoping that one day you'll be lucky enough to collaborate with a director who is truly inspired and actually gives you brilliant direction. Fingers crossed.

PART III
Reel Life

*It's your road, and yours alone. Others may walk it with you,
but no one can walk it for you.*
—Rumi

There is no one alive who is you-er than you.
—Dr. Seuss

Auditioning

As soon as I graduated from NYU, I moved back to Los Angeles to start my career. This was the mid-eighties, and as I began auditioning for film and TV roles, I was considered "too ethnic" for most parts. The lead roles were usually meant for blond-haired, blue-eyed, "American-looking" gals. I definitely didn't fit that bill. I would be cast as a Middle Eastern lady, a Colombian, an Italian, the devil, a dangerous, bad, mean girl—you know, anyone who had dark features. A girl once said to me that when I walk into a room, people assume I'm a bitch due to my arched eyebrows. I still don't totally understand that mode of thinking, but maybe it's written in some casting manual.

When asked about my ethnicity by a casting director, I would proudly tell the truth: "I'm a Jew from the Valley."

That always got a laugh, followed by: "No, really, what are you?"

When I would reply, "No, really, I'm Jewish on both sides," I'd hear back, "You don't look Jewish. You're too pretty to be Jewish."

It was mildly insulting, and definitely anti-Semitic. I'd be tempted to say how some of the most beautiful women I knew happened to be Jewish, but would instead just brush it off with a laugh, do the audition, and try to land the gig.

I was doing mostly theater then, and my ethnicity didn't seem to be a problem. I was excited to play characters of various backgrounds, religions, genders, even animals (my personal favorite). I was an actress, and it was thrilling to play something I was not. I enjoyed learning about different cultures and seeing the world from different points of view. I soon began saying that I was Belgian, Russian, or Polish, instead of Jewish—all true, by the way. Sometimes I'd throw in Spanish or Native American for good measure. I considered myself a woman of the world after all.

I basically started saying I was whatever the part was supposed to be. Back then, we all lied on our résumés. It was common practice.

"Oh, sure, I know how to use the trapeze—I took circus classes last summer."

"I'm an excellent horseback rider."

"Yep, I ride a motorcycle."

Do I speak French?

"*Oui!*"

It didn't matter. Once you got the gig, you would learn whatever skill or accent the role required. That was part of the fun.

One evening while I was waitressing at some restaurant, a drunk redheaded man asked me if I was an actress. When I said yes, he told me they were looking for a young woman to cast in a play by William Mastrosimone at a new theater downtown. He told me that I was perfect for the part. I scribbled down the information he gave me on the back of my orders pad. The next day, I brought my headshot and mostly fictitious résumé to the address he had given me and left them with the casting people.

Soon, I got a call—they wanted me to audition! It was for the part of Sherina in a new play called *Nanawatai*. The character was a spirited and rebellious Afghan girl during the Russian invasion of Afghanistan in 1979. I read the play and thought it was fantastic. I worked on the sides, and the next day went in and landed the part. I was jubilant. I was also so naive that when I learned it was an "equity" play (where they actually pay you), I sadly told them that I didn't have an equity card. They patiently explained that I could qualify for an equity card with this part. This was a big deal. It felt like getting the golden ticket, like the doors to Oz opening up.

And it was particularly exciting since the play would be appearing in a brand-new venue, the Los Angeles Theatre Center. Up until then, the Mark Taper Forum had been the only equity house in town. The cast was excellent: Steven Bauer, Philip Baker Hall, Adam Arkin, Tommy Swerdlow, and newcomer Bill Pullman, to name a few. I studied Farsi, hung out with and befriended a small group of incredible Afghan women who were also in the play. They graciously took me under their beautiful wings, and taught me their prayers, how to make their tea, and how to do their traditional dances. At one of their parties, they insisted I perform the marriage dance surrounded by the male guests sitting in a circle, watching me, evaluating me, deciding if I could possibly be their bride. I didn't feel comfortable at all, but the ladies said I had to do it, that it would be good to experience this traditional ritual. Even though they meant no harm, this all felt quite misogynistic to my Western sensibilities. In the end I obliged, not only to experience and embrace what my character Sherina might have felt, but also out of respect for these women who were letting me into their sacred community. Yet being objectified in that way, with men leering at me and cheering me on, made me feel humiliated and not very AlphaPussy at all.

Nevertheless, I loved the play and got excellent reviews. I thought I was on my way. But afterward, to my amazement, I could not get another audition to save my life. Even a casting director who had seen *Nanawatai* and thought I was great told me he was looking for an *American* girl. Once again, I was too ethnic. Too dark. Too "Middle Eastern."

What the fuck? Were these people dumb? I was ACTING. I had intentionally made myself look and sound and behave more Middle Eastern—I was playing an Afghan! Weren't they supposed to have some imagination? I was a surfer girl from the Valley, for fuck's sake.

A notable irony was that, later, when *Nanawatai*

was being adapted into a feature film, the casting department didn't want to consider me for the role of Sherina—she had to be Afghan, and I was too . . . American.

I basically forced my agents to get my foot in the door, and after I slayed both scenes in the audition, the producers were surprised at how good I was in the part—"You really understand her!"—at which point I must admit I got a bit snarky and thrust the Samuel French version of the play at them, pointing to my name on the cast list.

"I *created* the fucking part, of course I know it!"

Rule #1: don't make the casting person feel like a fool. I instinctively knew this, but I was pissed and hadn't yet mastered the art of masking my disdain. Also, they ended up casting an Italian in the role. So there went that excuse. And to be honest, they should have cast an Afghan girl to play Sherina. As much as I loved the part, that would have been the right thing to do in this case.

Several years later, Mastrosimone suggested me for the miniseries *Sinatra*, which I ended up doing, a project that I absolutely loved. So at least there was that.

My First B Movie

My career in film was not going well. I'd get little gigs here and there, audition a lot, but never seemed to be the right type. I wanted to play a lead in a film. A part with an arc, with some character development, not just a line here and there. Then one day I landed a principal role in a film! But don't get too excited, it was a lame movie that reeked of exploitation. Although I did like the character, just not the script. It happened to be a Roger Corman film, yet at the time I didn't get how cool that actually was—it just seemed like a super-dumb movie.

So many people—actors, writers, directors—had gotten their break with Roger Corman, King of the B movies. Even Jack Nicholson cut his teeth in Corman productions. Plus, my old teacher Martin Landau had been cast in the movie as well. He called to say how excited he was that we'd be working together.

"But Martin," I responded, "it's kind of a piece of shit, no?" I told him I wasn't sure it was a smart move to accept the offer. Yes, I wanted experience in film. But it was completely preposterous and of course had that obligatory naked moment in one of the scenes.

And it read like something worse than a B movie—more like a D or an F, if there is such a thing.

"Gina," Martin said, "even with bad projects, you can still work on your craft. Sometimes that's when we learn the most. You'll get paid. You'll be a working actor. Besides, it's going to shoot in the Philippines—they've been having political unrest, so it will be a very interesting time to go there. It'll be an adventure!"

Martin's words were persuasive and made me think I'd be an idiot to turn this down. Besides, if *he* was doing it, why shouldn't I? But I was still contemplating the scene where the two girls are so hot that they just have to remove their clothes in the middle of the bug-infested jungle to take a swim. You know, as one does.

Fortunately, I had a good lawyer and he explained how there's this thing called a "nudity clause" that would protect me from any unwanted indignities. In the case of this jungle scene, the clause he ended up negotiating stipulated that there would be a long shot and my entire body could take up only 30 percent of the entire screen, and would be shot from behind. Essentially, my tush would appear on about 5 percent of the entire screen—I could live with that. So off I went to the Philippines to shoot my first lead in a film, *Sweet Revenge*.

I figured this would be a good opportunity to make my character much better than it was written, thereby elevating the entire project. Well, as my hillbilly ex-boyfriend used to wisely say, you can't polish a turd.

In any case, I was able to practice David Mamet's "direct yourself" approach. At some point, due to the extreme humidity, our director wound up in the hospital with heat exhaustion. So now there was literally no director. One afternoon we were filming in the middle of the South China Sea, only to realize that the camera boat was nowhere in sight. No one could find the camera. It was a shit show. And we were using *live* AK-47s! Someone who didn't speak English would hand me the weapon . . . with the safety off. We were lucky no one was killed.

When the original director failed to return from the hospital, the cameraman—when he finally resurfaced—took over. I believe his only credits before this had been a couple of porn films. *Great*. Needless to say, by the time we got to the aforementioned jungle scene, I didn't exactly trust anyone. Maybe I was just being paranoid, but I really thought that instead of respecting the 30-percent-of-the-screen nudity deal, they would zoom in and make it a 100 percent body shot. Too much booty for my comfort. So, I came up with a plan to protect myself and the other actress, Michele, who was worried about the same thing.

I bought a red marker, and as we disrobed, preparing for the ridiculous jump into the lake—which, by the way, was murky as fuck, teeming with bugs that skipped along the surface—I told Michele to turn around. I promptly wrote *FU* on her left butt cheek and *CK* on her right cheek. Then I had her write *OFF* on my sweet cheeks and made sure I was standing to her right. If they decided to zoom in on our bodies, they would see a delightful message written across our lovely asses. Talk about sweet revenge.

One needs to exhibit some ingenuity if one is to survive the jungle.

I did, nonetheless, have some incredible experiences and adventures in the Philippines. I saw all of Imelda Marcos's legendary shoes on a visit through her abandoned home. (By the way, there were a lot of doubles of the shoes, or the same shoes in different colors—the whole collection not as extravagant as one was led to believe.) I got to watch Corazon Aquino, the new president, getting sworn into office, the successful outcome of a movement led by the People Power Revolution! I also snuck off to Hong Kong one weekend and fatefully encountered my past-life husband. So there was that. Lots of great life experiences that Martin had promised, though I was still anxious to get my career going.

Once back in LA, I continued to audition for parts that I wasn't blond enough, old enough, young enough, ugly or pretty enough for—you get the picture. There's only so much rejection a gal can take before feeling a bit down. I needed a break. I was starting to feel the one thing I promised myself I would never become: bitter. I needed to get back to my happy place—New York City.

Back in the Apple Again

I let my agents know that I needed a break from auditions (rejections), and was heading back to New York for a few weeks. Not that I thought they'd care, but it made me feel slightly powerful saying it. Like I was taking some control over my own life. They didn't argue, in fact they told me there was a play at the prestigious Long Wharf Theatre that I was right for, and as long as I would be in New York, they would set up an audition.

The play was *Camille*, starring Kathleen Turner. I was convinced it wouldn't happen, that I'd never get the part, but I went anyway and breezed through the audition. I wasn't nervous at all because in my mind it simply wasn't going to happen. There's the old philosophy, especially in acting, that when you truly let go of something—the desire or need to get a job, for example—it often comes flying at you.

Well, that's exactly what happened. After I exited the audition room and pressed the elevator button, the casting person came running after me telling me not to leave just yet—I had gotten the gig.

They were *running after me*. That never happens.

You usually wait around for weeks wondering if you'll be hired. Sometimes you can lie to yourself that you really don't want the job, but that's rarely the case. This has occurred only two other times in my career: when I got a job by detachment. And they were great jobs. I guess it really is some secret universal law, or else it's the acting gods being like, *Sorry, kid, you ain't quitting on us yet*. Or perhaps it was just fate.

While doing the play, I commuted back and forth from New Haven to New York via Penn Station. I was having a blast. It was a fantastic part. Janine, the guttersnipe who schemes and connives her way to the top, eventually takes over the role of Marguerite (Kathleen Turner) as the grande dame courtesan. Ron Daniels from the Royal Shakespeare Academy directed, and I absolutely loved working with Kathleen. She was a real baller. The brilliant David Hyde Pierce and I had a particularly comical scene doing a ridiculous dance. Working with David, I learned the skill of how not to "break" (i.e., crack up laughing) when your scene partner is beyond hysterically funny.

Speaking of fate, at the same time that I was doing *Camille*, a few friends—some from NYU, some from just around—decided to have a meeting to discuss forming a theater company. There were a bunch of us aspiring writers, actors, and directors who weren't getting hired as often as we liked (or at all). I'm not talking Broadway, but the smaller, more innovative off-Broadway and off-off-Broadway spots like the Ensemble Studio Theatre, Playwrights Horizons,

Cherry Lane, the Public—the places where the most interesting shows were being done.

So, when I was invited to this meeting, I went. I was instructed to bring something inspirational to read. I brought a passage from the great Rainer Maria Rilke's book *Letters to a Young Poet*:

> *You ask if your verses are good. You ask me. You have previously asked others. You send them to journals. You compare them with other poems, and you are troubled when certain editors reject your efforts. Now (as you have permitted me to advise you) I beg you to give all that up. You are looking outwards, and of all things that is what you must now not do. Nobody can advise and help you, nobody. There is only one single means. Go inside yourself. Discover the motive that bids you write; examine whether it sends its roots down to the deepest places of your heart, confess to yourself whether you would have to die if writing were denied you. This before all: ask yourself in the quietest hour of your night: must I write? Dig down into yourself for a deep answer. And if this should be in the affirmative, if you may meet this solemn question with a strong and simple, "I must," then build your life according to this necessity; your life must, right to its most unimportant and insignificant hour, become a token and a witness of this impulse.*

We had a few more meetings like this one, with a few more people gathering, and before we knew it, we were an official theater company: Naked Angels.

It was a seriously talented group that included Fisher Stevens, Rob Morrow, Bruce MacVittie, Ned Eisenberg, Kenneth Lonergan, Jon Robin Baitz, Frank Pugliese, Joe Mantello, Pippin Parker, Toby Parker, Jodie Markell, Nancy Travis, Jace Alexander, Nicole Burdette, and Jack Merrill, to name a few. Many other notable writers, actors, and directors joined along the way and played with us, too many too mention. Please look it up if you're interested. Or wait for the documentary that I'm sure will materialize one day soon.

Before long, we were becoming the groovy go-to theater. We eventually rented a huge space, around 5,600 square feet, from Jack's Uncle Carl. Predictably, we started having fantastic parties after our shows—I think we were the first theater with a velvet-rope door policy. We also made exquisite mushroom tea that we would drink in the basement at our fundraisers while trying to figure out how to handle the money. Fiscal responsibility was not our forte. John F. Kennedy Jr. came on as a board member. We were very happening.

My routine consisted of reading plays, rehearsing, building sets, performing shows, playing midnight softball, drinking at cheap dive bars until three or four a.m., going home, sleeping, then rinsing and repeating everything the next day. Life was sweet. Simple. These were the days when I could squeak by on five hundred dollars a month, including New York City rent.

We were doing our one-act plays for nothing, meaning: nobody was paying us, though we hoped our hard work was an investment in our future. And it was. Eventually. But at the time, Naked Angels was a place where we could have our own showcases, building a community while working on our chosen professions, all the while having a blast—and let's be honest, it kept us from going crazy. If you're an actor, you need to act. The same goes for any creative profession that you feel passionate about. One must create or else suffer the psychological and psychic consequences that NOT expressing yourself might have on your soul. Naked Angels certainly helped me decide to stay in New York, rather than return to Los Angeles. LA and I just didn't get on. She was not my lady.

One morning, my manager at the time—who had seen me in one of our shows and believed in me—told me about an audition for a small part in a movie that would pay ten thousand dollars for two days of work.

What?! Ten thousand dollars was a fortune to me and would take care of my life for almost a whole year. I jumped at the chance, worked on my audition, and was determined to get this gig, even though the movie wasn't any good and I wasn't that psyched about the star of the film. But it beat waitressing, and could feed my lifestyle.

The star, who was reading with people, was holding the auditions at his hotel uptown on Central Park South, which just happened to be next door to where my aunt and uncle were staying, and I was having dinner with them later that night. When my manager told me that she didn't want me going to a private hotel room for an audition, I assured her I'd be fine. I knew how to protect myself if need be. In truth, the circumstances were just too convenient. Audition, then walk right over to dinner. Two uptown birds in one subway ride. I'd be fine, I told her.

I announced myself at the front desk and made my way up to the penthouse. When I knocked, the star himself answered the door, pulling his shirt over his ponytailed head.

"Come in, come in!"

"It's okay—I'll wait out here until you get dressed." *Rude*, I thought, and let the door shut to give him privacy.

He immediately opened the door again, visibly annoyed.

I'm wondering, *Doesn't this guy have an assistant or casting person here?*

Nope. It was just him. *Red flag*. But hell—I was already there and dinner wasn't for another forty-five minutes. I stepped inside.

He asked me some lame questions, and once we got started, he kept interrupting my reading. And then . . .

"You are so cute—why don't you get up and walk around a bit?"

(Not that it should matter, but I was wearing Levi's, a T-shirt, and my all-purpose blue blazer. I looked a bit too conservative for the part, but was dressed perfectly for dinner afterward with my family.)

I instinctively replied: "If you're going to get weird, I'll just leave."

"No, no, no. Don't leave." He paused, looked at me intently, and said, "I think you should audition for the part of my wife, the lead."

Did he think this was going to get me all excited? Prompt me to skip around the room with glee? All that entered my mind was, *Oh, then I'll have to kiss you in the movie. No thanks.*

"Seriously," he went on, "sit down, sit down. You are so cute."

With that, I said, "I'm good. Best of luck with your movie."

I walked out of the audition knowing I had blown it. Or didn't blow it, so to speak. But I didn't really care—he was gross, and my instincts were leading my actions. I slipped away unscathed, ten grand out the window and me out the hotel room door.

Imagine my surprise when my manager called the next day to tell me I got the gig.

Really?

Maybe I'd misread the room and he was just testing me out for the role. The character was indeed feisty and didn't take any shit.

Huh.

My first day on the set—day one of two—I came prepared and ready to rumble. We were doing a scene in some bar with lots of extras. There was this one buxom woman with a very tight top, and the AC was on, so her nipples were alert. The star was blatantly staring at her. Then he said to me, as if I were his bro or something, "Would you look at those nipples? You could dial a phone with them."

"Excuse me?" I mean, what a weird thing to say. I was even trying to imagine it—I'm quite literal. But before he could make some other inappropriate comment, I turned to him and politely said, "We're going to get along great if you just don't talk to me."

I got up and headed over to the donut table, assuming I would be fired for this. He was, after all, the star and one of the "producers." I didn't care. He was a pig. I didn't need to listen to his crap.

Still, I wasn't fired. I finished the two days, took my money, and kept my dignity—well, other than the fact that I was embarrassed to be in that stupid film. I was just happy that I could buy a round of drinks for my teammates the following week after midnight softball.

Sibling Rivalry

I sometimes find myself getting carried away while I write these stories, as if the mercurial memory thread gets caught on one of the many folds in my brain—also known as *sulci*—somewhere in the temporal lobes where long-term memories are stored. It must be really crowded in there. I wonder if it's organized or looks like one of my desk drawers that always makes me think, *I really need to organize that drawer. Clean it out. Marie Kondo the shit out of it.*

In fact, I need to regain control of *all* of the drawers in my home. Sock drawer. Bathroom drawers. Kitchen drawers. Jewelry drawer. They are a fucking mess. Every new year has the same resolution: *This year I will get organized.* It's as if my mantras have dementia. Anyway, what was I talking about? Sorry, my nicotine patches and cappuccinos don't seem to be working today.

Okay. So . . . several years after my run with *Camille*, Jon Robin Baitz's one-act play *The Substance of Fire*, which we'd performed with Naked Angels, was going to be turned into a full-length workshop/

production and coincidentally performed at the Long Wharf Theatre in New Haven.

The original casting was Ron Rifkin as a patriarchal father who runs a publishing house, with Rob Morrow, Bradley White, and myself as his children who are attempting to take over the company. The play deals with family dynamics and generational trauma. Robin Baitz is an exceptional writer who really understands the unspoken—and sometimes spoken—tensions between siblings and parents. We were all glad to have the opportunity to keep exploring this piece. And we were even getting paid this time!

Most nights we traveled back and forth from New York on Amtrak, but on the weekends when we had matinees and evening performances, we were put up at the old Duncan Hotel in New Haven. Luxury it was not. Originally, it had been a boardinghouse. It had a run-down vintage charm about it, with a lingering smell in the tiny rooms that hinted at somebody's grandmother's chalky perfume and moldy carpets.

The play was difficult and constantly being rewritten—it was an exciting process, and we were all trying to do our best. One Friday, after a particularly challenging week, all I wanted was to pass out and get some sleep for the upcoming four-show weekend. Already in my pajamas as I was just getting into bed, there was a knock at the door. It was Bradley, who whispered urgently from the hallway, "Gina, it's me and Rob, open up, we need to tell you something!"

Oh no, I thought, *did someone die?*—my go-to disaster possibility. The moment I turned the knob, they came bursting through like a pair of psychotic hyenas and pulled my mattress, cardboard pillows, scratchy sheets, and blanket off the box spring, dumping everything on the floor. Then, screeching with glee, they fled the scene of the crime. Are you fucking kidding me?! That was uncalled for and, needless to say, ridiculous. I tried to put everything back together, but the mattress was simply too heavy for a young thespian such as myself to lift. And this wasn't the type of establishment where you could call someone for help.

I had to sleep and that bed wasn't going to move on its own. So I went to Rob and Brad's room to tell them to come back and fix my bed. I knocked, but there was no response. This wasn't cool at all. It brought up feelings from when I was young and my brother and sister would gang up and mercilessly tease me. I knocked again, harder. "Guys, c'mon, open the door."

Old memories of being locked out of the room when my siblings were hanging with their older friends started to bubble up. It was like I was eight all over again. It also reminded me how they would cruelly hide my beloved blankie, whose softness against my cheek, combined with my delicious thumb-sucking, would rival any drink-and-drug combo today. They would torment me, stealing my totem of security, and when I'd hysterically bellow through snot-nosed tears, "Where's my blanket? Give me back my blanket!" they would sadistically taunt: "Baby! Baby! Baby!"

To my relief, Rob and Brad finally opened the

door, but then, to my shock, they threw a bucket of water at me, soaking me in humiliation, before slamming the door in my face. Their hyena laughter mocked me even more.

I felt rage boil deep within my body—*Give me back my blanket!!*—as I turned and squished my way back to my room. I hadn't done anything to invite such cruelty. Sure, we were playing antagonistic siblings—but let's be professionals and leave the fucking dynamics on the stage.

I needed to rise up, avenge this heinous action, make them pay for stealing my blankie . . . or, rather, my dignity. But what to do?

There were two of them—bigger and probably stronger. I didn't have any weapons on me, thank god, because I just might have used them. Rage is blind. Rage knows not of common sense. Rage's only friend and adviser is revenge. I needed to be clever.

But what . . . what . . . *what* . . . ?

Suddenly, my eyes landed on the plastic bottle of Dr. Bronner's peppermint soap I had packed for the weekend. I suited up in my army-like jacket, grabbed the liquid weapon, slipped it in one of the large pockets, snatched my big tube of Tom's spearmint toothpaste for good measure, and shoved it in the other pocket. This was war.

Stealthily, I moved back into enemy territory.

Knock knock knock. "C'mon, guys, open the door," I groveled. "Please, I need you to put my bed back. You won, okay?"

More vicious laughter from the other side.

"Please?" I was trying to sound as vulnerable as possible.

The door opened a few inches and Brad peeked out.

I tried to push in and the two of them pushed back. But I am no novice—I jammed my foot in the door and cried out that they were hurting me . . . my foot was getting crushed! Rob and Brad debated whether or not I was acting, and as they let up on the door just enough to release my hoof, I smashed through with all my might—ha ha, I *was* acting!—wielding my soap and paste like some Western gunslinger.

I squeezed hard and targeted anything and everything—their bed, their clothes, their open suitcases, and apparently Rob's eyes (which I swear to this day was not intentional). When I had successfully achieved my mission, I triumphantly walked back out the door and told them to go fuck themselves.

Sure, I had to face the consequences—sleeping on a mattress sprawled on a potentially bug-ridden carpet—but it was worth it.

To this day, Rob and Bradley are still like brothers to me. We joke about it. I loved them then, I love them even more now—but a gal has to defend herself when need be.

Players

I always loved Robert Altman's movies, including classics like *Nashville*, *M*A*S*H*, and *3 Women*—he was a hero of mine. When I found out that he was casting a movie called *The Player* about a Hollywood studio, and that it had a particular part for a young story editor that I felt I could do justice to, I asked my agent to please get me a meeting.

Unfortunately, the film had already been cast. My agent suggested that I go meet the producer Scotty Bushnell, who cast all of Altman's films. That way, I'd have my foot in the door for future projects. It sounded like a good idea and arrangements were made.

The morning of the meeting, I put on a flattering white blouse and my English jodhpurs. As I was waiting for Scotty in her office, Robert Altman himself passed by in the adjoining hallway. Our eyes met for a quick moment, then he kept walking.

A few seconds later, he turned around and stepped into the room. "Who are you?" he asked.

"I'm Gina Gershon."

He pointed to my jodhpurs. "Do you ride?"

"Well, I don't really ride horses, but I play them." I had no idea that he was into betting on the ponies.

We started talking about gambling and racetracks: Santa Anita versus Hollywood Park, different jockeys, certain horses, handicapping, and betting strategies. Well into our conversation, Altman said, "What are you doing here?"

"I'm actually an actress. I love you as a director and I really want to work with you. I was hoping to be considered for the role of Bonnie in *The Player*, but I understand Cynthia Stevenson already got the part."

"Have you ever been in anything?" he asked.

"I just did a John Sayles movie—*City of Hope*."

"John Sayles—I like him. Do you know how to improvise?"

"Yes, it's my favorite thing!" This was a lie—I'd never done improv in my life.

He told me they'd be shooting from July 1–14. "For those two weeks, why don't you just come and be in the movie?"

"For which part?"

"We'll just make it up," he said.

"Really?"

"Sure!"

"There's only one day I can't work during those dates," I told him. "One of my best friends is getting married and I'm a bridesmaid."

"Good to know. We'll just keep you out of that day . . . How about we make you an assistant to Bonnie—but you really want her job. Do you like the name Whitney?"

"I do."

"We can call you Whitney Gersh."

And that's how I got that gig.

Working with Altman was an incredible experience. I would just be sitting around watching the action and he'd say, "Okay, kid, give me something." I'd blurt out whatever came into my mind based on what was happening in the scene.

Altman would give every actor separate recording tracks to go along with their microphones—hence that signature naturalistic feel where everyone is talking at the same time. He was undeniably one of the pioneers of this technique. He liked what I was coming up with, so he started giving me more to do. One day, he called me into his office. He was typing when I entered.

"Hey, kid, take a seat." He indicated the chair next to him. "Have you ever seen *Touch of Evil*?"

"Yeah."

"Well, that movie has one of the longest tracking shots ever filmed. About three and a half minutes. I'm gonna beat that. Our opening will be around eight minutes long, introducing the players and the studio, all filmed in one tracking shot."

As he was talking, I noticed he was also typing Whitney Gersh into the scene. Up until that point, my character hadn't been in the actual script—just improvised. He then explained the scene and said that it would take one day to rehearse and one day to shoot—the longest single shot ever; it would be historic.

"You want to be in it?"

"Uhhh, yeah!"

"There's only one problem."

"What's that?"

"Well, we rehearse all day that Friday, then we'll shoot it all day Saturday. I'm not sure exactly how long it'll take to get it, but once we start, you won't be able to leave. It's the Saturday of your friend's wedding. I'm a man of my word—and I told you that you could have the day off. It's totally up to you: if you can't be in it because you have an obligation, I understand; but if you do want to be in it, it's going to be very cool, though you'll most likely miss your friend's wedding. It's up to you."

Luckily, my great friend still to this day, Jill Goldman—the one getting married—happened to be a filmmaker herself. When I told her the dilemma, she sadly but emphatically said, "You *have* to be in that scene!"

So I did the scene and went to the party after the wedding. Thanks, Jill.

Altman wanted everyone to be part of the process. I remember one scene that he was really struggling with; he kept pacing back and forth, trying to figure it out, then he turned to me and said, "This isn't working. Got any ideas?"

This really floored me.

I was flattered that he respected me enough to ask my opinion, and then realized he would have asked *anyone* who was standing next to him. That's how self-assured he was as a director. It's the really confident ones who will listen to anyone who has a good idea. I've learned the hard way that more often than not, a director who is super rigid is usually the same director who is very insecure ... and often not as brilliant. Of course, there are exceptions.

Altman also encouraged everyone to come and see dailies. It felt very communal. Making a movie can sometimes be so isolating, and this was just the opposite. Plus, there was free pizza. Altman would take it a step further and have gatherings at his house on the beach, which might include treats like performances by Annie Ross or Lyle Lovett. Some of the best weed I'd ever smoked would be passed around. Altman really knew how to build a community while he was making a film. I love *The Player* and still discover fantastic new details every time I watch it. I'm just so happy and feel so lucky that I got the opportunity to work with the great Robert Altman.

Thank god I wore those jodhpurs.

It's funny how I've worked and worked and strategized to get certain jobs, but then some of my favorite gigs ever have materialized in the most unexpected ways.

In 2003, Denis Leary asked me to be part of his roast. I had never been to a roast, let alone participated in one, but since Denis is a much-adored friend, I said I'd be happy to join. He wanted me to sing a song, and of course say a few words.

"What kind of a song?" I asked. "What kind of words?"

He said he'd get the song to me and that I could say whatever I wanted.

But then . . . with three weeks remaining before the show: no song.

Two weeks till the show: still no song.

Four days before the show, I started to get worried.

"Don't worry, you'll have cue cards."

"Denis—it's live! I'd prefer to know what I'm doing. I'm a rehearsal kind of gal, especially when I'm singing."

"It's a pretty long song, it'll open the show," he told me, but he kept vacillating between genres: "It'll be a rock and roll tune. No . . . blues. No, I'm thinking it should be punk."

"Denis . . ."

Two days before the show: "Sinatra style. And you'll have dancing cigarette girls. Or should I say, girls dressed as packs of cigarettes who happen to dance."

Sure.

My costume was an ode to Judy Garland when she performed "Get Happy" in her 1950 movie summer stock—fedora, blazer, sheer tights, heels. Snazzy. Now, a few words, hmmm, what to say? I ended up preparing a little speech about how much I loved Denis, how he was like a big brother to me, how much nicer he was than his persona, etc. It would be genuine and heartfelt.

I was up first. I was nervous and would have preferred more rehearsal time, but whatever. I did my bit and it went alright. As soon as it was over, I immediately had a shot of tequila and smoked a ciggy to calm my nerves. *Phew*. Glad that was over. Just then, one of the production coordinators came into the green room and told me we had to do the number again since my fedora had been too low and my eyes were shadowed. *Shit. Why didn't anyone catch this in the dress rehearsal?*

"Okay," I said, being a trouper, "let's do this right now before the tequila kicks in."

"We can't do it now," the guy said. "The show is live, so we have to wait until the very end and redo it then."

"Oh, you mean after two and a half hours, when the audience is dying to go home?"

"Yeah, then. Sorry, we can't stop the show. You can come and watch in the audience if you like until you're up."

"Sure, why not." I decided it would be better to enjoy the show than get tense for two hours in my green room all alone. So I joined my wonderful friend and writer extraordinaire Richard LaGravenese, who was drinking and laughing, having a great time.

After about two minutes, one of the guys onstage started talking shit about *me*! Did I mention I was the only woman on the roster? The rest were a bunch of dudes: comedians, firefighters, actor friends. One after the next, they started making cheap *Showgirls* comments and other crude remarks intended to get cheap laughs. *What the fuck?*

Richie said, "Honey, it's a roast—that's what they do."

"Yeah, but I'm not the one being roasted, Denis is!"
"It's a free-for-all, baby. Anything goes."
"Well, nobody told me that!"

I take some responsibility for being so damn naive. Maybe I should have watched a few of those old Dean Martin and Frank Sinatra–type roasts.

I had another tequila. Then another. By the time I went on again, it is safe to say I was a wee bit tipsy, and a wee bit more than angry at all these guys taking cheap shots at me. I told the second assistant director to vamp a bit before my song—I was changing my monologue. *They want a roast, I'll give them a fucking roast.*

I went after every guy on the dais, spewing out whatever came to mind. I don't even remember what I said; I just let the tequila speak. Then I began the song.

What was once a swingy Sinatra-like vibe, I suddenly turned more into a hardcore rock-and-roll rant. I let my emotions (and alcohol) guide my artistic impulses.

After my number, Jeff Garlin, who was the master of ceremonies, came up to me and said it was the funniest thing he had ever seen. I *had* to be on *Curb Your Enthusiasm*, the TV show for which he was both a lead character and a producer. They would call Monday.

But all I heard was, *Blah blah blahity blah*. I was still simmering in my annoyance.

Come Monday, I got the call.

"If you'd be willing to play a Hasidic Jew one more time, we'd love you to come on the show this week." (I wasn't aware that I had ever played a Hasidic Jew.)

It was a very busy time for me: I was starting a new movie, doing a photo shoot, press for something else, etc., etc. So I wasn't sure it would work. Besides, I had never seen *Curb Your Enthusiasm* and had no idea what it was all about. Fortunately, on that Monday I happened to be hanging out with my friend Rick Rubin, who told me, "If there is only one job you do all year, it should be *Curb*."

Rick is a smart guy; I valued his opinion. So I said sure. I'd make it work. But I knew nothing about being a Hasidic Jew—I needed to do some quick research.

"Don't worry," Rick said, "you'll just be playing yourself. That's what they do with celebrities on that show. You'll just improvise. Trust me, you'll be glad you did it."

When I got to the set, I was told the Hasidic woman I'd be playing worked at a dry cleaner and had the hots for Larry David, who appears as himself on the show and is also its creator.

Larry asked, "Can you do some sort of nondescript accent?"

I immediately thought of my waxer, Rochelle: she had a mishmash accent of French and Israeli, with some Bronx sprinkled in. "*Larrrry*," I whined.

He laughed and said, "Perfect." And then we improvised one scene after another. It may be the most enjoyable time I've ever had on a set. Rick was right. I was so glad that I did this. They ended up writing Hannah—my horny Hasid—into two additional episodes.

So once again I can thank my outfit—in this case the fedora, which by some divine intervention shadowed my face—for helping me land one of my favorite gigs ever.

Emotional Detachment

I had never been to an astrologer. Horoscopes in the papers and magazines were, in my opinion, for suckers. They were so general and broad that any vulnerable dupe going through a rough patch could read some charlatan's forecast and think, *Oh my god, that is so ME!*

Despite this bias, however, in June of 1994 I decided to gift myself a reading with an Indian man named Chakrapani. A friend of mine swore by him, and seeing that I was in a bit of a slump, I was open to anything that might help me through my existential crisis. I was told that Chakrapani was amazing at predicting someone's future according to when, where, and the exact time they were born. He was an astrologer, not a psychic. Astrology uses the position of the stars and planets to help determine your life path, as opposed to a psychic reading, which is based on intuition and clairvoyance (and is, in my opinion, much more unreliable).

I had just split up with a boyfriend whom I was wildly in love with, my career was going absolutely nowhere, my so-called agents were losers, and to use my great-aunt Ida's favorite phrase, I didn't have a pot to piss in—in other words, I was broke. It felt extravagant spending 150 bucks on some stranger who was going to explain my past and advise me on my future. As it turned out, it was the best possible use of my food allowance.

I had always felt a connection to the metaphysical. My first paying job had been playing a spirit to my sister's mystic. Tracy was nine, I was four. She would wrap a schmatta around her head, post a sign that said, *World-Famous Spiritualist,* and enlist me as "a being from beyond our earthly realm." She made me put on a bikini and then she'd cover me in toxic, glow-in-the-dark paint and hide me in the closet.

As I've mentioned, between my brother and sister, I was subjected to what was essentially psychological warfare when my parents weren't around. And much to Tracy's chagrin, she had to share a room with me and would always kick me out when she had friends over. Or when she wanted to do her homework. Or brush her hair. Or listen to music. Or breathe. Basically, I was allowed to sleep there. Nothing else.

Today, I am very close to Tracy, she's the greatest sister a gal could ask for, but back then she could be an absolute bitch—a bitch whose love and approval I coveted. Which is to say, I would do anything she asked of me, just to be included.

Anyway, my sister would charge my parents' dinner-party guests fifty cents to witness the Great Spiritualist at work. Seated in the dark, with only a small flashlight illuminating her schmatta-covered face, Tracy would ask the spirits to knock three times if they were present.

A professional from the get-go, I took my direction and would boldly knock three times from inside the closet.

Tracy would then command with the authority of Max von Sydow in *The Exorcist*, "Spirits, show yourself and dance!"

At this point, I would come out of the closet and do my best impression of a possessed dancing spirit—flailing arms, gyrating legs, and then a sudden disappearance back into the closet until the show was over.

I'd take my cut of ten cents out of the fifty-cent entry fee Tracy was charging and feel pretty good about myself. This job clearly served as foreshadowing to life as an underpaid performer.

Nonetheless, in that moment, I was living the dream, being included in anything *Tracy*.

Fast forward to 1994: Chakrapani started to tell me about all of these planets—the positions they were in and how they affected me—yadda yadda. I was sitting there waiting for him to get to the good stuff. What was going to happen with my career? My love life? The basics.

He went through what he called "a bird's-eye view" of my life—from my early years up until now. I must say, he was pretty darn accurate. He spoke of traumatizing timelines that weirdly coincided with big events in my family—when we moved out of the Valley and away from my friends, when my beloved cat died, and when my father passed away. Impressive.

"But what's happening now, Chakrapani? What's happening *now*?"

A concerned expression crossed his face. He said something about the Rahu in the Youtoo in Uranus and other meaningless drivel.

I interrupted and asked him to please use language I could understand. He then told me, in a very ominous tone, that the months of October, November, December, January, and February "push you up like nobody's business—but it is very stressful. Can you handle the stress? I do not know."

I perked up. "What do you mean? Is this a job you're talking about?"

"Yes," he said, "a big job. The sun is in position to shine on you so the whole world notices."

"Well that sounds great!" My skepticism vanished and I was instantly feeling more optimistic than I'd been in months.

He looked at me like I was an idiot. "*Is* it great? Why is it great? I do not know. The pressure is big and your mind is not at ease."

I came to realize that Chakrapani could give a shit about fame and fortune; he was only concerned about my mind being at ease. My soul being calm and at peace. As the years have gone by, I've come to see that there was wisdom in his words—but at the time, I was just excited that a big job might be headed my way. Who cared about being at ease?

"Listen carefully to what I say . . ." Chakrapani

had lowered his voice to an intense whisper. "The only way you will ever get through this period is by practicing emotional detachment. Without emotional detachment, things will not be favorable for you."

Yeah, right. That made no sense. This crazy fortune teller obviously didn't grasp how mercurial and intense show business could be. I thought it best to share my contrasting view: "Chakrapani, when I'm acting, I can hardly be emotionally detached. It just doesn't work that way. If I'm working, I need to be open to my emotions." *Duh.*

At this point, Chakrapani began shouting: "EMOTIONAL DETACHMENT IS THE ONLY WAY YOU WILL GET THROUGH THIS WITH EASE! DO YOU UNDERSTAND ME? EMOTIONAL DETACHMENT!"

Okay, okay, okay!

A vein in his neck was threatening to burst and I didn't want to cause an old man to have a heart attack, so I simply responded, "Yes, got it. I understand. Emotional detachment."

I left there thinking he was a total nutcase.

A few months later, I won the part of Cristal Connors in *Showgirls*. Rehearsals were to begin in October, with the filming commencing in February.

It wasn't until late December that I realized exactly how prescient Chakrapani's words had been.

"I Think I'll Call You Ghee-na"

So there I was in an S&M bondage outfit, hanging by a rope sixty feet in the air, waiting for my cue, watching a bunch of naked people dance below me, thinking, *How the fuck did I get here?*

I had studied the classics. I wanted to do Chekhov. I dreamed of playing Masha, Medea, Mary Tyrone. Instead, it felt like I was in some terrible TV show, *Survival of the Tittest*.

We were about a month into shooting *Showgirls* and the absurdity of the situation was really starting to hit me. What had begun as a dream role was turning into a gig that could potentially end my career before it even got off the ground.

I remember being so excited when I first got this job. I had always been a huge fan of Paul Verhoeven's Dutch films: *Spetters, Soldier of Orange, Turkish Delight* . . . These were all outstanding films with that groovy European feel. The kind of movies I loved. And here I was, about to step into the role of Cristal Connors, a character I envisioned as a dark, twisted fusion of Margo Channing from *All About Eve* and Aphrodite from the Psyche and Cupid myth.

It was the follow-up film from the writer/director team who'd brought us *Basic Instinct*. In my mind it was going to be like a Wagner concert: complicated and intense. I would utilize my years of classical Greek drama training and bring this very complicated, tortured woman to life. The story would be set in the sleazy, low-lit underbelly of Las Vegas nightclubs, oozing with blind ambition and compromised morals. I fantasized about the movie having subtitles in French. Or better yet, Dutch. Making it feel edgy and sophisticated in a cool, pretentious way.

As I looked down upon the scantily clad chaos below, I realized that I had gravely miscalculated the situation. This was no Wagner opera. It felt more like some Technicolor nightmare version of a teenybopper pop concert. I kept hearing snippets of the Talking Heads song "Once in a Lifetime": *My god, what have I done?* This was crazy-pants. How the hell was I going to come out of this alive? And when I say *alive*, I mean come out of this able to work again. I had big hopes. Big dreams. So my career at the time certainly felt like a life-or-death situation.

At that very moment, the door to the stage burst open, and a guy with peroxide-blond hair, in an orange plaid suit, video camera in hand, sauntered in, filming as he surveyed the situation. My first thought was, *That guy is going to save my life.* I was lowered down and I did my dance, then walked straight over to him, extended my hand, and said, "Hi, I'm Gina."

"Hi, I'm Dave," the wacky dude replied. And like that, a beautiful friendship was born.

I may have been literally hanging from a rope, but at this point, mentally, I was hanging from a thread. I had never met Dave Stewart—best known alongside Annie Lennox as the band the Eurythmics—but my soul immediately sensed in him a long-lost tribe member. Dave had been hired to replace the music that Prince had sent over. Thank god. I hate to say it, but it wasn't great, and I don't say that lightly. I adore Prince's music, and he was rightly considered a god among musicians and artists alike—so original and so insanely talented. I was a huge fan. Once, I'd even had a very unusual encounter with him . . .

It was my first year at NYU and I was busy producing and starring in *Antigone*, as well as performing in a production of Tennessee Williams's *This Property Is Condemned*. Out of the blue, I got a call from Jill Jones. She was the beautiful, sexy girl in the cap singing, "*I was dreaming when I wrote this, forgive me if it goes astray,*" in Prince's "1999."

Jill and I had gone to Beverly Hills High together and performed in several musicals. I remember how backstage at our senior musical, *The Music Man*, she told me that she was hanging out with Prince and was totally into him. I was impressed: "You're seeing a *prince*?" I had no idea who he was.

A few years later, I was certainly aware of him and how brilliant he was when Jill called and said, "Prince wants to meet you. He's doing a movie and the lead woman has to be able to sing, dance, and act. I told him about you. He wants to meet you."

"Well that's fucking awesome!" I responded. "Thanks, Jill, this could be the perfect first movie for me."

"Great. Can you come to Minnesota tomorrow?"

"What? No, I can't, I have a show tomorrow night." (Note that when I said *show*, I meant doing our little production in some black-box student theater. But still, I took my commitments seriously.)

"Well, what if you fly over afterwards, then go back the next day in time for your show," Jill proposed.

I figured that would be indulgent, but also exciting. It was a chance to star in a movie and sing with Prince. Oh my god. "Sounds great!"

In the Tennessee Williams play, I was portraying a young Depression-era girl living in a condemned building. I had dirt on my face, pigtails in my hair, and an old thrift-store dress. As soon as the show was over the next evening, I raced out of the theater, hopped into a taxi, and headed to the airport.

By the time I reached Minnesota, the dirt on my face had been replaced with black-kohl eyes and very red lips. My pigtails had been released and my hair teased within an inch of its ratty life. My little dress had been swapped out for a tight black leather miniskirt, fishnets, and a bright pink shirt. This was the 1980s, folks.

When I stepped off the plane, there was a purple stretch limousine waiting to pick me up. I had never even been in a limousine before, let alone a purple one. Jill jumped out, gave me a big hug, and introduced me to the Artist Still Known as Prince. He was *little*. I immediately slumped down to not seem too tall. And he was shy. And really cute. And oozing sexuality. We said hello and got in the back of the stretch.

We stayed there on the tarmac making small talk, until he said, "Would you like to hear the title song of the movie?"

"Oh yes, please!"

I was sitting to the left of Prince, and Jill was on the opposite seat, facing us. There was a large moonroof above, letting in a beam of light from the runway. Prince pushed play.

As you can imagine, the sound system was amazing. By the time the first chorus of "Purple Rain" hit, I had chills running all through my body. You'd have to be a tone-deaf, music-hating mongrel to not recognize the absolute brilliance of this song. It was so wonderfully orchestrated and arranged. I got quite emotional. And as if the moment couldn't get any more magical, when the second "*Purple rain, purple rain*" chorus landed, a light rain begin falling through the open moonroof, morphing into a slight mist spreading into the limo, as if a fairy-dust sprinkler had been turned on. I almost started crying, it was so beautiful.

When the song ended, we all sat in silence. I couldn't speak at first, I was in awe. After a bit, I began breathlessly babbling about how genius it was. Perhaps that was some sort of test I unknowingly passed, because Prince then told the driver it was okay to get going.

We left the airport and went someplace I can't even recall. We drank, we talked, we danced, and after a while Prince and I were more comfortable with each other. I was going on with some lame story and he was staring at me in such a way that made me stop talking. It was as if he was developing some grand scheme in his inspired brain.

After a few moments he said very quietly, almost to himself, "I think I'm going to call you Ghee-na." (A hard G sound: as in *gi*—what one wears in karate; or *ghee*—what hippies eat instead of butter.)

"Ghee-na?" I responded. "As in Ghee-na Gershon?" I was trying not to laugh.

"No," he very seriously said. "Just Ghee-na."

The night went on from there. We went back to his purple house, where he played the piano and we sang. He did funny Rick James impersonations that made me laugh some more. I was really having a great time. He gave me the script to read. He gave me his room to sleep in, and I was amazed how comfy his bed was. I guiltily looked inside his closet and admired his collection of platform shoes.

In the morning, however, I told Prince that after reading the script, I knew it wasn't for me. I wasn't sure about the sex scene, and secretly didn't love what ended up becoming Apollonia's song and character in the movie. But truth be told, he lost me at "Ghee-na."

Back in *Showgirls* land, I'd initially been bummed when I was told we weren't going to use Prince's music, but the universe works in mysterious ways. As it turned out, Dave Stewart became one of my best friends and a very influential person in my life. We've had many amazing adventures all around the world together. But more importantly, he kept me relatively sane during the filming of the movie. We would recap the day and exchange bizarre moments we had witnessed. He would serenade me on his guitar as the makeup artist powdered my ass. It was such a blessing to have a kindred spirit present, reassuring me that things were, in fact, as crazy as I thought they were.

Many times I have regretted not working with Prince. I would kill for the chance to have been able to make music with that genius. But I didn't love being controlled. And the way he looked at me as he said "Ghee-na," it was as though invisible ropes were snaking around my wrists and throat, threatening my artistic sovereignty. I was uncomfortable with the idea that I'd be called that for the rest of my life. Something just didn't feel right. And what ever happened to Apollonia? All I know is that even back then, a struggling student in college, for better or worse, I listened to my instincts and turned down what sounded like a fantasy job.

Over the years, Prince's need to completely control (and in some cases destroy) the people in his life has been revealed and documented. Doesn't take away from the fact that he is and always will be regarded as a musical genius.

This Will Destroy Your Career

Only actors themselves know if they connect to a particular part—if they can truly play it. It's a feeling in one's gut. When I've read a part that I really love—that I know I absolutely *must* play—the character jumps off the page and grabs me by the throat. That's how it had been with *Showgirls*. Cristal Connors got under my skin from the very first *darlin'*.

I knew exactly what to do with Cristal, the unapologetic, complex, and fierce diva. She *belonged* to me. But my agents at the time had different plans. They were really into me acting in . . . wait for it . . . *Friday the 13th: The Final Chapter*. What was it about that franchise? It kept popping up in my life like some greasy drug peddler offering me Ajax-laced cocaine.

On the day of my final callback for *Showgirls*, my agents had wanted me to go meet the producers for *Friday the 13th*. I tried to tell them that *Showgirls* had the potential to be a big movie. Paul Verhoeven was a cool director. If the movie worked, it'd be totally fun, and I knew I could really do something exciting with the part. So I went to the callback for the movie that

I liked. I figured that even if it were to fail, it would still be more spectacular to do than some slasher film.

I had given my phone number to Johanna Ray, the casting director on *Showgirls*, just in case my agents tried to sabotage the project in hopes of getting me to sign a contract for the next five *Friday the 13th*s.

Needless to say, I left those agents and went over to a more established agency when I got cast in *Showgirls*. At least the new guys understood why I wanted to do the movie and were excited about and supportive of the prospect. They seemed much smarter than the last ones. I've always dreamed of working with the same team—agents, manager, lawyers, etc.—throughout my career. People who know what I'm about, are aligned with my goals, respect my vision, and truly want what's best for me. I was hoping these new representatives would be that.

One year and countless traumas later, there was a lot of buzz around *Showgirls* and my new agents were trying to land me a big studio picture. I liked the way they were thinking, but I kept telling them we needed to get a new movie ASAP, before *Showgirls* actually came out, because I was afraid it might be a disaster. I needed a movie without all the glitz (and tits) to show that I could really act—something completely different.

Then this new script was sent to me to read. It was called *Bound*.

I recognized the writers' names immediately: the Wachowskis. They had written a script called *Assassins* that I loved; I had really wanted to be seen for that part, but no dice. Whatever the reason, casting wouldn't bring me in. They were, however, very interested in me coming in for *Bound*.

The script did not disappoint. I had never read a woman's part like Corky. She reminded me of roles in some of my favorite movies. Marlon Brando in *On the Waterfront*, Montgomery Clift in *A Place in the Sun*, Robert Mitchum in *The Night of the Hunter*. You know—the male parts. The heroes. The guys who ride off into the sunset with the girl after triumphing over evil.

Bound was like a classic noir film, except this time the romance was between two women. And Corky was the character who not only got the money and the car, but did in fact get the girl as well. She was the complete opposite of Cristal Connors. What a relief it would be to cut off my hair, cut off those fucking nails, and wear very little makeup. I was eager to say these lines and bring this fantastic script and character to life.

Alas, my new, enlightened agents told me there was no way they would let me do it. It was an independent movie, not the big-budget studio film they were going after, and most of all it was a (*gasp!*) "lesbian movie." No one in their right mind would let their client do it.

"I just want to go to the meeting," I pleaded. "At the very least I can talk them into letting me audition for *Assassins*. They are great writers, I really want to meet them."

My agents reluctantly set it up.

The last thing I wanted to deal with was what I'd experienced with *Showgirls*. I was really hoping for a movie that I didn't have to maneuver and manipulate my way through. When I walked in and had my first conversation with Larry and Andy Wachowski (soon to be known as Lana and Lilly, respectively), I could feel this was a very different type of situation. I asked them all kinds of questions about what the movie was really about, what were they trying to say, how they were going to shoot certain scenes. They had never directed anything before, and just because someone can write, that doesn't mean they'll be a good director.

Every answer they gave blew me away. They were clearly visionaries. I got that crazy feeling in my stomach that only activates when I'm around incredibly gifted people. I was sold; I told my agents I was in.

Again my agents said there was no way they were going to let me destroy my career by doing this film. I had just played a lesbian in *Showgirls* and it would hurt my prospects to do it again. I argued that Cristal wasn't a lesbian, she was bisexual (this whole conversation is so antiquated now), and that they shouldn't reduce *Bound* to a "lesbian movie." This was a film about trust, and the character just happened to prefer the ladies.

"So she likes women. Who cares?"

Well, apparently Hollywood did. My agents threatened to stop representing me if I did *Bound*.

They left me no choice but to drop them. I was very disappointed and saddened by this. I told them that they would get the commission but I was going elsewhere for future representation.

I am honored to have been a part of *Bound*. I'm proud whenever girls tell me how important it has been to them. How it helped them come out of the closet. I'm proud that Larry and Andy, bound in their male bodies, were brave enough to transition into Lana and Lilly, the women they always were inside. The Wachowski sisters are both brilliant, beautiful, and so talented; I couldn't love or respect them more.

The movie came out, and then, within a week, it was basically gone. Distributors stupidly promoted it as a lesbian movie. If it weren't for critics like Siskel and Ebert and columnists like Liz Smith who stated that this was one of the best films of the year—if it weren't for DVDs where people could actually *see* the movie—*Bound* would have disappeared. Not because it wasn't a well-crafted film made by exceptional filmmakers, but because of the relationship between two strong, clever women in love.

Today, playing a lesbian isn't frowned upon, and in fact it can win you an Oscar and lead to a wide variety of great parts. But thirty years ago, things were different. And while I hate to admit it, maybe my agents had a point, because after *Bound* came out, even though I got extremely positive reviews for my performance, I was mostly offered the roles of tattooed psycho lesbians who rode motorcycles and had predilections for murdering men. Still, I'm happy that I listened to my gut and did that movie, which has become one of my all-time favorites.

Snatches of *Showgirls*

Let me begin this saga by saying that I don't like to lie. I am not fond of liars. I do not like them and will not tolerate lying in my professional or personal relationships. Ever since my dad instilled in me that there was nothing I could do that I would ever have to lie to him about, I've made it a priority, for better or worse, to be as honest as I possibly can. This credo of integrity, however, is basically impossible to follow when it comes to getting a gig in Hollywood and doing good work on difficult projects. And, of course, if you've actually read this whole book, you know there have been times when I've, well, bent the truth a bit, though I don't think I've ever done so to be malicious—just out of the necessity of the situation.

One of the reasons I hate Wikipedia and IMDB: their tendency to not tell the truth by botching 50 percent of the "facts." They very rudely feel it necessary to list my age, which is often wrong. How many siblings I have, wrong. My romantic relationships, consistently wrong. Although it's amusing to see who I've been linked up with—and how could I have not known that I have a daughter named Julia??

* * *

While visiting Papua New Guinea on a diving trip with some fabulous friends (I love how pretentious that sounds), I had decided to give up the notion of age. It just made me feel old. Or anxious. And limited. In Papua New Guinea, I had absolutely no idea how old the Korowai people (also known as the Kombai) I encountered were. It probably helped that they didn't have mirrors. Several times I tried to ask, best I could, when someone's birthday was or how old they were, but they would just look at me like I was crazy. I couldn't for the life of me tell if the guy standing before me was the father, son, or grandfather.

Except for when they'd smile—I figured the guys with the missing teeth were the elders (and the ones with the red-stained lips were high on betel nuts). Or when the boobs sagged down to a woman's waist— probably the great-grandmothers.

Still, age didn't seem important. Everyone worked in the village equally, as far as I could tell; ability was all that mattered. When I showed some Korowai photos I had taken of them, it was an incredible thing to witness. They pointed at each other and giggled in amazement, and none of them seemed to be judging themselves or each other. It made me wish mirrors didn't exist.

After that trip, I thought, *Fuck it, I'm not going to think about my age anymore because it doesn't matter. What matters is my state of mind. Who really cares anyway?*

Apparently, a lot of people. Especially if you're

a woman. And it doesn't help if you're an actress. In America, ageism is alive and well.

When I first met Sharon Stone, she inspected my face and informed me that I looked younger than my thirty-one years. She advised me to start lying about my age. She warned me that after forty, they stop sending you scripts, and suggested I begin lying now to get ahead of it. I naively stated that I didn't want to play that game, that I'd be cast on my merits as an actress. Sharon smirked knowingly at that.

As it so happened, in the case of *Showgirls* I did lie about my age. Ironically, I needed to be *older*. I felt like I was too old to play the seemingly innocent, Eve-like newbie, Nomi Malone, but too young to be the hard-bitten, seen-it-all, Margo-like star, Cristal Connors.

I believe I told the producers I was thirty-four or thirty-five years old. To me, Cristal had to be at the end of her career, closing in on forty, in order to feel threatened by Nomi, the ambitious newcomer. I worked hard to present myself as this reluctantly "maturing" showgirl. I stuffed my bra to look like I had fake double-D's; I caked on pounds of makeup to age up a bit; I even changed the timbre of my voice and rhythm of my words to sound like a jaded Southern diva—I really wanted this gig. When I walked into that first audition, I was already in character. I had to make them believe I *was* Cristal Connors.

After two months of intense auditioning, acting out the scenes—I'd had three or four callbacks at this point—they were finally going to teach me the choreography for the dance routines. This was what I'd been waiting for. I had been dancing since I was fourteen and knew I could crush that part of the audition. My confidence was boosted further when the choreographer, Marguerite Derricks, showed me the main number, a Bob Fosse–like sassy dance to "Money" by Pink Floyd.

Yes! Fosse was my jam!! I'd even auditioned for him once.

I had just finished college and I'd never had a professional dance audition before. I thought it might be fun. I had read about the gig in *Backstage*: there was an open call for a Broadway production of *Sweet Charity*. What the hell.

I had no idea who would be there. I grabbed a coffee and headed off to some Broadway rehearsal room. There were soooo many people there waiting to audition—I signed in at number 683. Yikes! It was going to be awhile, so I went out for an Egg McMuffin to kill some time.

When I got back, I heard George Benson's groovy version of "On Broadway" playing behind the closed doors. After the first sixteen bars of that undeniably great riff, the music stopped and the dancers who were auditioning came out of the room—a few smiling ear to ear, a few with the unmistakable look of dejection. It was just like in the movies.

They were letting five girls in at a time. When they called number 645, I started to get nervous. I knew all we had to do was a jazz-walk across the floor to make the first cut. As some buxom-blond cutie—clearly a seasoned hoofer—walked out of the room, I asked her who was in there. I didn't even know who was directing it. She looked at me like I was a total moron and snippily replied, "Bob Fosse, you ever heard of him?"

I stopped breathing and went into a bit of a panic. Fosse was my favorite choreographer. I couldn't believe I was going to dance for him. Oh my god, I wasn't *that* good. I raced into the bathroom and bouffed out my hair, pushed up my tits, threw on some lips, then headed straight into the audition room, oozing as much sex as my young body could muster. I figured what I didn't have in technique, I could make up for in attitude.

Not only did I get past the first cut, I made it down to the final fifty. At the end of the day, when they were teaching us three new dances to learn for the next callback, Fosse himself—cigarette dangling iconically from mouth—came up behind me, put his hands on my hips, and showed me exactly how to move. I was in heaven.

The next day, I nailed the famous Frug number and did okay at the more modern routine. Yet when it came to the ballet part, the dance captain, already annoyed that I was still there, looked over to Bob as if to say, *Have we had enough?* (I really suck at ballet.)

Fosse shrugged his shoulders and offered me a little smile that said, *I tried*. I gave him a respectful salute back and walked out the door, feeling good about my only professional dance audition.

Until *Showgirls*.

* * *

Which bring us to Lie #2.

After months of auditioning and waiting, the big day came when I would be putting my dance on tape.

I was feeling confident—so cocky, in fact, that I didn't get there early like I intended, and had to jump right into the audition without properly warming up.

It was all going great, I was slaying it—until I got to the right high kick, which I could land next to my ear on a good day. As I enthusiastically kicked my leg high and hard, I heard what sounded like a very loud rip. I stopped suddenly and asked, "Did you hear that?"

"No, I didn't hear anything," one of the casting people said. "Please go on."

A voice in my head told me not to continue or I would hurt myself beyond repair. Something in my body had definitely ripped. But I knew that if I admitted this, I'd most likely lose the gig. They'd think, *How can she handle fourteen-hour dance days if she can't even get through an audition?*

Fuck.

Without thinking much, I simply played the diva card—very Cristal Connors of me—and nonchalantly explained, "I don't feel like dancing right now. I'll come back later." I haughtily left the room without waiting for a response. I was on video, mind you, so I stayed in character and tried not to limp.

As soon as I got to my car, I burst into tears. I knew something was very wrong. It just so happened that Elizabeth Berkley was there on the street—I can't remember if she'd been given the part of Nomi Malone yet, but we had already done a reading together. She came right over to see if I was alright. I confided in her and we bonded immediately. She was very sweet and seemed genuinely concerned.

I immediately drove to a chiropractor—a reputable sports guy named Dr. Hacopian who a friend highly recommended—crying the whole way, knowing that I had probably lost the part. I couldn't believe I'd told them I didn't feel like dancing. *Oy*.

Well, Dr. Hacopian informed me that I had ripped the shit out of my hamstring and wouldn't be able to dance for at least six weeks.

"No way," I responded. I had to be able to dance on it in more like *three* weeks. I had gotten a role in some crappy movie being shot in Ohio and figured I could dance for *Showgirls* when I got back—if they'd still have me. "I'll do anything necessary, Doctor, just fix me!"

Thus began an intense process of exercises and ultrasound therapy. With sheer will and lots of physical therapy, my leg healed in just three weeks, though credit is also due to a stuntman on the set of the Ohio movie who would painfully massage my torn hamstring, breaking up the scar tissue. Let me tell you, that shit was painful. I've never appreciated ultrasound more. The elegance with which it quietly and painlessly breaks up scar tissue, making sure your torn muscles can heal without any repercussions in your later years, is what has gotten me through all my many injuries. And no, I don't own any stock in it, although I seriously wish I held the patent.

My hamstring healed, I got my groove back, and when the *Showgirls* casting people allowed me to resume my auditioning, I nailed the dancing.

I was taking a bath in my tiny apartment on 12th Street in Manhattan when the phone rang. I picked up and it was Johanna Ray, the casting director. We chatted for about twenty minutes until the bathwater started to get cold, and I finally summoned the courage to ask her what was happening with my audition. "Oh darling," she said, "the part is yours! I'm sorry, I thought I already told you."

I remember hanging up and sitting quietly in my tub with a big smile on my face until all the water had run down the drain. Wow. Johanna had told me I'd be working for five months total—two months of dance rehearsals beginning in October, then three months of actual shooting, concluding in February. Chakrapani's voice echoed in my brain: *October, November, December, January, February . . . pushes you up like nobody's business . . . Can you handle the stress?*

I've always had a hard time watching *Showgirls*, and not for the obvious reasons that most actors with any shred of perfectionism have when watching their own performances. Sure, upon any first viewing, I'm always consumed with dread. I pick myself apart. My face, my voice, my choices, etc. I start to think about other professions that I could pursue. Becoming a dream psychologist for children used to always be a consideration. Or perhaps an interior decorator like my mother. Maybe even a flamenco dancer in Spain.

But the primary reason I have a hard time watching *Showgirls* is my accent. It is completely off at times. Sometimes not even there. I pride myself on being able to do a pretty decent accent when the role requires it. In fact, I love accents. It says so much about a character. Not only where they are from, but their social status, their level of education, little flaws in their psyche—the voice and how we speak, consciously or unconsciously, reveal way more than people often realize.

So I was very excited to find Cristal's voice. Given the fact that she says *darlin'* every other page, and that she is introduced as "the Yellow Rose of Texas," it would make obvious sense for her to have a Texas twang, which would also make some of those dumb lines easier to say.

With this in mind, I had my first "inspired idea" on how to introduce my character. The first time we see Cristal, she's doing a press conference. When she gets back to her dressing room, she washes her face, removes her false eyelashes, and tells her assistant to go get her something. She has had a nose job and, like most of the showgirls in the movie, a boob job. My idea was to reveal how much of a true facade Cristal actually puts up: fake boobs (she'd pull out some padding), fake face (she'd wipe off the much bigger mouth), fake hair (she'd take off a half wig), fake nails (she'd pull them off), and here's the kicker—

when alone in her room, speaking to her assistant, Cristal Connors would have absolutely NO Texas accent. Even her voice would be fake, therefore her whole persona has been made up—genius! I was so excited to share my brilliant idea with the director, Paul Verhoeven, knowing that he, too, would love it.

Wrong.

As soon as I enthusiastically suggested how fabulous the no-accent moment could be, a look of slight horror fell over Paul's face and he very sternly said, "No accent. I don't want anyone to use any accents in this film. Use your own voice. Absolutely no accents."

Holy shit. You have got to be kidding me.

"This part doesn't work without an accent," I said. "She's the Yellow Rose of Texas, for god's sake—I *must* have an accent. This is a great opportunity to reveal so much . . ."

But he was adamant: no accent.

So here we are at Lie #3

I told Paul it was fine, I'd just use my own voice. Then I casually mentioned I was originally from Tennessee and this was the way I talked. I realize I should have said something like, "It's so weird, I'm from Texas, just like Cristal," but my sister lived in Nashville at the time and it's what popped into my head.

Did I mention that Paul is Dutch? Well, I gambled that he wouldn't be able to discern the vocal nuances of American Southern accents: Texas, Tennessee, what's the difference? A lot, actually. So, when I landed on an accent that belonged to a stripper I had met from some small town in Texas, I hoped he wouldn't know the difference. I mean, can you imagine all of those *darlin*'s without an accent? *Quelle catastrophe!*

Yet sneaky as I was, I still hear every little twangy mistake when I watch the film. Usually when you do an accent in a movie, you have a dialect coach to keep you on point, plus you can tweak the dialogue in postproduction with ADR (automated dialogue replacement). Not in this case. I couldn't ask Paul to let me fix any word or phrase because my accent was off. He would have gotten too angry that I had lied to him, and by postproduction it just wasn't worth another battle.

So to this day, I can't watch the film without cringing every time I hear an accent mishap. Which happens more times than I'd like to admit, darlin'.

Know Your Line

I do love playing complex characters—trying to figure them out, the seeds of their struggles, what they think they want, what they *really* want, etc. I found one of my greatest teachers in the legendary Sandra Seacat. Under her guidance, I was able to apply new techniques for figuring out my characters, and thus expanding my own essence—integrating my "shadow self" into my day-to-day. It's crucial to determine why we do what we do, what triggers us. Through dreamwork, shadow work, and active imagination, my understanding of both myself and my roles has grown. Besides, it saves tons of money that would usually go toward therapy when I work this way.

I have been fortunate for the tutelage of other great acting coaches as well. I love working with Sandra's daughter, my fellow classmate and great friend Greta Seacat, who is simply one of the best out there. Plus, I got to work with the late Harold Guskin, one of the most outstanding coaches ever, with an entirely different approach to character. (I encourage you to read his wonderful book, *How to Stop Acting*.)

I like flawed characters because they are so interesting to figure out. I don't believe that anyone is born bad. Even Rhoda in the film *The Bad Seed*, one of my childhood favorites, is finally discovered to have had a maternal grandmother who was also a murderer—thus begging the whole nature-versus-nurture question. But I digress. Again. (Adderall, please. Actually, these days I use nicotine patches for focus. With Adderall, I can write for hours and hours, sure, but it makes me quite cranky and unpleasant to be around. Just saying.)

I'd take what I learned from both Seacats and Harold, mix it with the advice from David Mamet about learning to direct myself, and make it my job to figure out my character's path. I'd map out the scenes, know what I was after—or what was secretly driving my character, what triggered them consciously or unconsciously—and then, when I got to set, I'd try to just be present and hopefully let it all flow.

I don't want to rely on the director to tell me what to do. If they have real insight or a clear vision for how my character helps the story, I am totally open. But like any good Boy Scout will tell you: Be Prepared.

Between my training and the guidance I got from my teachers, I put in the work. Beyond just digging into the "whys" of a character, I loved stepping into another world—trying to understand how they lived, what their days looked like, what they dreamed about. If you stay open, the answers are everywhere. It's like living in a waking dream—full of symbols and hidden clues.

* * *

In preparing for the role of Cristal Connors, I started going to all kinds of dance venues and strip clubs. To be honest, I'd been going to these kinds of places for years. From the mid-eighties and into the nineties, New York was peppered with all sorts of shady late-night establishments, such as Billy's Topless on 22nd Street, New York Dolls Gentlemen's Club on Murray Street, and the Harmony Burlesque in Tribeca, which in 2013 turned into one of my favorite yoga studios, Lyons Den Power Yoga. And, of course, peep shows were alive and well all around the sleazy 42nd Street district, before Rudy Giuliani came in, "cleaned it up," and turned it into a tourist-friendly megawatt shopping mall.

The women who worked in these venues had always fascinated me. Who were they? Why did they do this for a living? Did they enjoy it? The Baby Doll Lounge, located right in the heart of old Tribeca, was one of my favorite spots. Very low-key. Very downtown. It was about three blocks from the courthouse and right around the corner from the First Precinct police department, so most of the clientele were cops and lawyers—not that they were in uniform, but their cars with the special laminated parking permits were sprinkled all up and down White Street. Felt like the safest place around—you didn't have to worry about outbursts of violence like in some of the Midtown joints.

There was a girl in her early twenties who worked at Baby Doll and danced with a baseball cap covering half her face. She was very sexy and seemed really into it—always in her own world, barely noticing the customers watching her. When I asked her why she was doing this job, she told me she was going to NYU and needed to make tuition. Then I asked how the job was affecting her, and she laughed and said, "I just look at these guys as if they're giant wallets. They mean absolutely nothing to me."

I believed her. Other dancers, more often than not, were single mothers, able to make more money at the club than at a nine-to-five job, and it allowed them to spend more time with their kids because of the relatively short hours.

I found it enlightening when going on location, living in an unfamiliar environment for months on end, to visit the strip clubs in the vicinity. I'd also go to the flea markets to check out the vibe. Between these two enterprises, I would get a sense of the place. The attitude, the customers, what the dancers were wearing—it all gave me clues about the ethics and culture of the town.

So now, years later, I found myself having to do a little research. It brought me great glee to turn in my late-night receipts from all these places of ill repute to my business manager, because guess what? Now they were tax write-offs! I interviewed strippers and showgirls, and one night I found Cristal Connors's accent in a bathroom at a topless bar in Las Vegas. The woman's voice rang like crystal—a frequency of wisdom, seen-it-all confidence, and something else I couldn't quite place. I struck up a conversation and asked where she was from—Texas. *Bingo*. I asked her how long she'd been a stripper and what led her to this line of work. She was a single mom, had been a teacher before moving to Vegas, couldn't make ends meet, and found that stripping was a way to earn a lot of cash at night and have the day dedicated to her child. In certain clubs, she told me, they paid even more to dance completely nude. I asked her if she'd ever done that.

"Oh, honey, no. I keep my panties on. My privates are between me and my boyfriend and God. Everyone's line in the sand is different and that's their personal decision. My line is this: I keep my undies on. It's important to know your own line."

With that, she left the bathroom for the stage with an air of dignity emanating from her like pure copal incense. It was a waft that protected her from the boozy, cheap, dubious environment. She inspired me not just in terms of Cristal, but also in my own life.

Know your line.

I was drawing and dreaming and collaborating with Ellen Mirojnick, the wonderful costume designer on *Showgirls*, whom I'd work with again on *Face/Off* a few years later. We had figured out almost everything, down to my last nail jewel and diamond ring. I was ready. But when I eagerly stilettoed my way onto the set that first day, I soon felt like I had stepped into a sparkly sequined sinkhole.

Doggy Chow

The first scene that was going to be shot was when Cristal takes Nomi (Elizabeth Berkley) out to lunch at Spago. Cristal has taken an interest in this new dancer. They begin to have, in my humble opinion, the dumbest conversation ever to occur between two sober characters:

> *Nomi: Don't they have brown rice and vegetables?*
> *Cristal: Do you like brown rice and vegetables?*
> *Nomi: Yeah.*
> *Cristal: You do?*
> *Nomi: Sort of.*
> *Cristal: Really?*
> *Nomi: It's worse than dog food. It is!*
> *Cristal: I've had dog food.*
> *Nomi: You have?*
> *Cristal: Mmm-hmm. Long time ago. Doggy chow. I used to love doggy chow.*
> *Nomi: I used to love doggy chow, too!*

The night before, I had called Paul Verhoeven to

make a plea to lose the doggy chow lines. No dancer I'd ever come across would have reduced herself to eating dog food. Pizza, yes. Ice cream, yes. Surely there was something else that could bond these two gals. It just didn't seem truthful, and frankly, I was still under the impression that I would be participating in something along the lines of Paul's dark and brilliant Dutch films.

"The line stays as is!" Paul snapped.

"It's really stupid," I said. "It makes them both seem like idiots."

"We are not changing one word of the script. And remember—no accents!"

I immediately called Harold Guskin and told him the situation.

"Who gives a fuck what Cristal says?" he responded. "You're fucking with Nomi. Start barking, have fun with it, don't take it so seriously. See how Elizabeth reacts—that's the fun part. The whole script is ridiculous. Your character shouldn't give a shit. The more ridiculous it gets, or however silly Elizabeth acts, just play with it."

God bless Harold. With that direction, he unlocked and freed me. So I took a 180-degree turn with ol' Cristal. I was going to make a fun character who the drag queens would dress up like on Halloween! Goodbye Margo Channing, hello Aphrodite.

I was now prepared for anything. I was going to have a great time. I was ready!

Or so I thought.

The Seven-Thousand-Dollar G-String

When I was fifteen years old, my best friends and I were very into modern dance. We'd prance around wild and free—toes pointed, midsections contracted. We loved Pina Bausch, Martha Graham, Merce Cunningham, and Bob Fosse, and we didn't think twice about twirling our taut teenage bodies around in the nude if the choreography required it.

So it wasn't that big of a deal to me that I'd be dancing partially naked in *Showgirls*. In fact, I was getting off pretty easy. For two of the three dance numbers, I was essentially covered up. The S&M outfit was a bit racy, but still not too extreme—except for that bondage bra with exposed breasts that I was planning on painting bright red to match my lips.

I couldn't believe how much money they were willing to spend on my costume. Yes, I understood that I was the title star of the Riviera Vegas show called "Goddess," but seven thousand bucks was a *lot* of sparkle. My costume would be a naked mesh bodysuit, covered head to toe in beautiful crystals, sequins, and other materials that would make a magpie salivate. It took three different fittings and many hours of a skilled seamstress sewing in one jewel at a time to create Ellen Mirojnick's vision. The form-fitting nylon would cling tightly to my body, from my toes all the way up my neck. The effect of the gold, red, and bronze crystals would be stunning—a fiery, elegant costume for the goddess when emerging from an erupting volcano.

It was the day before one of the numbers was to be filmed. There were around six hundred extras and we were going to perform it just like a live show. Everyone was excited and nervous to reveal all the work that had been done—from the choreography, to the costumes, to the hair and makeup design. Hopefully Paul would like it.

After nailing the first run-through, we were psyched that almost everything had gone as planned—it felt like the piece was really starting to gel. My costume, however, wasn't totally working. Paul said it looked like a floating head on top of a sea of jewels. I could understand that. So we started cutting away at the neckline, to open it up a bit. We saved the extracted material and thought it would be a nice embellishment in my hair.

A five-hundred-dollar headband—why not?

We did the number again and filmed it this time, so that the camera crew could get used to the moves—I believe we had five cameras set up to catch every angle far and near. Ellen came up to me after the second run-through and said the costume was still not looking quite right—we needed to chip away at it some more.

I was getting a bit anxious because I still wasn't

cleanly hitting a few of my turns. Due to my perfectionism, all I could think about was getting this thing right before tomorrow. Annoyed at how long it was taking to cut away some of the fabric on my body, I suggested we just mark it up so I could take it off and we could keep working out the number uninterrupted. At this point, I was very comfortable with everyone around me. Besides, all the other dancers were only wearing G-strings.

I stripped down and we continued rehearsing.

I got to the set early the next morning excited to perform. I had run through the choreography all night in my head (a great way to rehearse, by the way) and couldn't wait to film it. The number was going to be great.

When I got to my dressing room, Paul and Ellen were already there waiting for me with unreadable expressions on their faces. *Oh shit,* I thought, *am I fired?* They sat me down and explained that when they watched the footage of yesterday's rehearsal, everyone unanimously agreed that I looked better and more graceful in just the G-string, not the whole bodysuit. Paul showed me a playback so I could see for myself.

Well, I couldn't argue with them. Somehow the whole piece was more effective when I wasn't so covered up. Being topless in this dance piece wasn't overly concerning to me, and besides, I would never be in this excellent shape again—if you can't feel good about yourself after dancing fourteen hours a day for three months, you never will. I figured it would be something I could look back on when I was an old flabby bubbe and show some whippersnapper the footage and in my best old-lady-from–Annie Hall voice exclaim, "I was once a great beauty!"

So they wanted to cut up my gorgeous costume into a very expensive G-string. Fine. I suggested I still use the jewels on my body and incorporate golden body paint just so I felt like I still had a costume on—it would make me feel less self-conscious and would look pretty cool. They agreed.

I adored David Forrest, my makeup artist. Not only was he fantastic at what he did and very fun to collaborate with, he didn't bat an eye when I started losing it, doing "bits" to maintain some semblance of sanity—like greeting myself in the mirror with a big Gloria Swanson–like "Hello, you!" and speaking in an extreme grande dame–esque sort of way.

Look, whatever one needs to get through the day.

David and I got along just great. Often your makeup artist will become a bit of a confidant on a set, especially when everything seems absolutely bonkers. So I felt perfectly comfortable asking him to help me design Madame Connors's boobs. We figured we could color in the nipples with a lovely rosewood pencil and glue lots of crystals and rhinestones all around the rest. When in doubt, ladies, bejewel! And bejewel we did. We even added highlights and shadows for that enhanced silicone look. Who knew Krazy Glue works so well on nipples?

So there we were one time, about four in the morning, handsome David on his knees before me, making sure my red rhinestone was perfectly centered on my nipple like a cherry on top of a scoop of vanilla ice cream, when he casually mentioned that he had been the Cowboy in the fabulous disco band the Village People.

Wait . . . WHAT?? How had he not told me this before? Talk about burying the lede. The guy bejeweling my tits had sung and danced to "Y.M.C.A."—I should have been bejeweling *him*. Now, I don't recall if he said the *original* Cowboy or if he came later, but I had never even considered that performers could be replaced without the fans knowing about it. Oh, I was young and naive then. This was before Destiny's Child, Menudo, and other bands that famously switched up their singers. I was well aware that people were pushed down the stairs and had to be replaced (it was right there in the script), but at least everyone knew the original performer had been supplanted by another performer with a different name and a new identity. But to just blatantly exchange one person for another and pretend it didn't happen? Well, it made us all seem so replaceable. (*Oh, hello, AI.*)

So let me get this straight—if you groom your hair the same way, put on the same outfit, and dance the same steps, no one will notice the difference between you and some other guy? You are like a cookie cutter, fitting neatly into someone else's vision of beauty and grace—very "Number 12 Looks Just Like You," which was one of my favorite episodes of *The Twilight Zone,* hands down one of the best series ever to be produced. If you have never seen it, do yourself a favor and check out *The Twilight Zone*, season five, episode seventeen. Rod Serling was a visionary and a genius. This particular story was written by John Tomerlin and adapted from Charles Beaumont's 1952 book *The Beautiful People*. It's basically about how everyone in the future wants to look like everyone else. Everyone else who is *pretty*. As Serling says in his opening narration to that episode, "*Imagine a time in the future, where science has developed the means of giving everyone the face and body he dreams of. It may not happen tomorrow, but it happens now in the Twilight Zone.*"

Hola . . . it *has* happened!!

So many people in today's world try to conform to whatever standard of beauty happens to be on trend. Everyone wants what's in: big butts, big boobs, big lips, big eyes. They want to be forever young. You need look no further than the incredible Kardashian tribe, who have set the standard for artificial beauty for a whole generation.

Cut to many sweaty hours later, when a few precious jewels had been rubbed and ripped off my body, and my nipples were so raw and red they looked as though I had been nursing triplets. It hurt like hell, but hey, the show must go on! So my dear David was on his knees once again before me, gently applying Neosporin to my tortured teats, along with more glue to replace the escaped rhinestones. As the old saying sometimes goes: *Oh, how we suffer for our art.*

Bedazzled Bondage

In order to crystallize Ms. Connors (sorry, couldn't help myself), I would spend hours on hair and makeup. I wanted her hair to be reminiscent of two of my favorite bombshells: Rita Hayworth and Brigitte Bardot. Luckily, we had the wonderful Marie-Ange Ripka to give me the perfect 'do. Height, volume, and pizzazz.

The makeup was an even more extravagant endeavor. Let me just say how much I like making up my characters' faces. You can change *everything* to suit your role. I remember doing mask work in school—I cherished the freedom of expression it gave me. The weirder, the better. With *Showgirls*, we were so lucky to have David as the makeup artist. He would shade my nose to make it look like it had been straightened and thinned out a bit, no problem. Then he would overdraw my already pretty full lips and emphasize the bow. I would put a touch of red on the inside of my lower lip while highlighting the rest of my lips to make them seem plumper and bigger, adding some gloss for a slightly fake look.

Believe it or not, my mother—whose lips all the

Gershon ladies inherited—taught me these tricks (except the glossy fake part). She would tell me and Tracy, "Girls, you must learn how to build your lips," which is still a running joke in my family. In fact, when she died, my sweet cousin Joanna gave Tracy and me lipsticks with *Build Your Lips* engraved in gold on their cases. I really miss my mom. She would spend an hour every morning putting on her gorgeous face. Just for fun, she once took a job at the makeup counter at Neiman Marcus, her favorite playpen. She had a great time applying makeup to random customers.

On set, we'd carve out my cheeks and add highlights to make it look like I had filler in them. But the most shading was done to my chest—lots of shading, highlighting, and padding galore to make my boobs look like they'd been bought. We decided it would be fun to add crystals to my upper eyelids for a bit more something-something. It actually made my eyes look bigger.

Our motto became "More is more." I was extremely happy with the look, even though it sometimes took a good two or three hours. I'd use that time to get into the mood of the scene. In my mind, Cristal never ate much, though she did like her cocaine. Champagne and coke, luncheon of champions. She does coke a few times in the movie, and since I was working with this Goddess Aphrodite vibe, I designed a coke ring that Cristal would always wear. One of the joys of a big-budget movie is that you can actually design shit for your character. I'd long held a fascination with poison rings. Since ancient times, some nobility, as well as spies, would wear these fancy jeweled rings with secret compartments that contained poison, so with a sleight of hand one could secretly dose their victim to death. In Cristal's case, cocaine was her poison. Not necessarily to share, but I wanted her to always have it on her—whether she was doing a bump or not.

In the Spago scene, I thought Cristal should be coked up a bit, so I used my time in the chair to do my sensory work and get into that good-time party mood. I was definitely feeling it, locked into Cristal, excited and ready to kick some ass.

And then Paul walked in. "You ready to do the scene?"

"Yeah, I'm psyched. Can't wait."

"And you are going to say the doggy chow line?" he pressed.

"Yeah, of course, no problem. I worked on it and really love it now."

"And you are going to do what I say?"

"Yeah, sure, Paul, it'll be great." I was really trying to keep my "high" up, but what felt like a passive-aggressive interrogation was starting to become a buzzkill.

Then he said something like, "Do you want to have a good life?"

"Yes, of course."

"Then you will do *exactly* what I say."

"Okaaaaay . . ." I responded, feeling invisible ropes weaving their way around my hands and throat.

Paul's lips began to thin—weird energy had replaced the jovial mood. I noticed everyone else had left the makeup trailer.

Stay with it, I told myself, *stay with the high, keep the good feeling*, but my inner panic threatened to overtake my actor's preparation.

When I was about six or seven, my brother Dann and I would play a game called "Houdini." He would tie me up with bathrobe belts from my knees to my shoulders, then I'd hop into the next room and slither out of them. I would reemerge, throw the belts at Dann, raise my arms in triumph, and chirp, "Ta-da!"

One day, he must have made the belts extra tight. I couldn't escape, try as I might, and instead of untying his little sister, he hung me upside down on his chin-up bar and left me there. It wasn't until my mother got home a little while later that I was discovered, slightly woozy to say the least. That was the last time I played Houdini with Dann.

It's fair to say that I am not a fan of bondage games. I go into a slight panic at the mere thought of being tied up.

As the tension mounted between me and Paul, it was like those invisible ropes were tightening on my throat. Despite my best efforts to maintain my party-girl vibe, I just exploded. Next thing I knew, I leaped up in my barely-there ensemble and, with a primal banshee scream, threw the chair across the room. Or, rather, that was my intention. Fancy makeup chairs in nice movie trailers are *heavy*. So when I tried to throw it across the room, it landed with a pathetic thud only a few inches away. Tears were now running down my face, several hours of makeup and emotional preparation wasted.

"Why are you doing this to me?!" I screamed. "I am an actress, just a Jew from the Valley trying to make a great character for *you*! Why are you doing this?"

Paul looked utterly astonished.

"Now we're going to have to redo my makeup! I won't be ready now for another two hours!" I'm a natural producer when it comes to making a film, very aware of falling behind schedule.

Realizing he had gone too far, Paul quickly left the trailer so I could get ready. Again.

I later found out that someone had set me up (I will not mention who). This person was telling Paul that I was being mean, doing things that I was not doing. So maybe Paul was reacting to that. Who knows, who cares. I went out and nailed the scene. Maybe all that toxic energy bubbling underneath my fabulous veneer added a little texture.

All I knew was that this was my first actual talking scene of the shoot. And, as it turned out, it was a typical day—with behind-the-scenes backstabbing and a constant psychological tug-of-war between Paul, Elizabeth, and me. This was clearly going to be a very long shoot. Paul was infamous for fighting with his stars, and—lucky me!—I guess I was his chosen sparring partner on *Showgirls*. This would be just the first of many battles.

Out-Crazy the Crazy

Paul and I were soon fighting constantly. It shouldn't be a surprise that this guy wasn't afraid of confrontation. Me: I hate it. Clearly Paul thrived on it. It's apparent in his work. When *Starship Troopers* came out, he didn't say publicly that it was an anti-fascist film, which it definitely is, and he got off on people's outrage when they thought it was pro-fascism.

When *Showgirls*[*] was up for seven Golden Raspberry Awards (the exact opposite of Academy Awards; these celebrate the *worst* in movies that year), Paul was the only director in "Razzie" history to gleefully show up to accept his award in person. By the time he'd collected all seven awards—thank god I wasn't included in any of them—he was smiling ear to ear, absolutely triumphant in his victory.

---

[*]Readers will notice that *Showgirls* appears in this book more than any other film I've been a part of. This is not because Cristal Connors was my favorite role; it's more because my experiences making that movie best capture my evolution as an AlphaPussy—both what I had already absorbed by that point in my life as well as the additional lessons learned during the making of the film. And to be honest, there were so many insane moments and stories that came out of the project that I could write a whole damn book on that movie alone. But for now, I'll just stick to all things AlphaPussy.

I think Paul secretly enjoyed it when we argued about the most mundane things. Sometimes I suspected he was throwing things out there just to see if he could get a rise out of me. Or maybe not. Maybe it was annoying that I didn't just roll over and do what he asked.

Whatever the case, our battles were becoming exhausting. And let me say this: I liked Paul. A lot! Especially when we weren't locked in some game of control. He is a very smart, very interesting guy. A mathematician and theologian. I really enjoyed our chats about religion and philosophy.

One day, we were scheduled to shoot a scene that was to take place in Cristal's dressing room. I believe it was when I was supposed to be getting my legs waxed. That turned into a shaving scene for some reason or another. In any event, I was in the hair and makeup trailer once again, waiting for my team to transform me, when Paul came in and said without any warning, "In today's scene, I think it would be good if you showed your vagina."

Whoa, that came out of the fucking blue. Just that morning I'd made a deal with myself that no matter what, I would avoid all arguments that day. Oh boy, this one was going to be a doozy.

"Why?" I asked. And in my most sincere, calm-actress voice, without trying to provoke or sound like an asshole, I continued, "I mean, what's the reason Cristal would do that? I'm open to anything as long as it makes sense. How does it reveal my character? How does it move the story forward?"

"Well, basically, Sharon Stone showed her vagina,

Elizabeth is showing her vagina, so I think you should show yours, too."

Remain calm. Stay cool. This isn't in the contract, I assured myself. *I can call my lawyer.* "Hmmm. Can I think about this for a moment?"

"Sure, I'll come back," he said, and left the trailer.

Look, I couldn't just bluntly say what I was thinking, because I was trying to prevent World War III. My interior monologue went something like, *No fucking way! Are you out of your pervy Dutch mind? There's absolutely no good reason for me to do this. It's completely gratuitous. It's not gonna happen.*

I went ahead and called my lawyer. I told him what was going on and he assured me that there was no way I had to do that. My contract very clearly stated what was agreed upon, what I had to show and what I did not have to show, and my vagina was definitely on the no-show list.

I was slightly frantic when speaking with him, to say the least.

Then I felt an ominous presence behind me. Michael Myers? Freddy Krueger? Nope—it was Paul. He had somehow snuck back into the makeup trailer unnoticed. *Oh shit.* Had he heard my conversation? Was he going to murder me?

I immediately hung up the phone.

Paul's lips were taking on that tense, thin look, which was now a tell that we were about to go into battle. My body tensed. My breathing got shallow. My mind started racing.

Out of nowhere, I heard Chakrapani's voice echo

in my mind: *Emotional detachment* ... Oh my god, was this what he was talking about all those months ago?

I excused myself, saying I needed to go to the bathroom. I steadied my breath, gathered my wits, and upon my return I evenly suggested that we discuss what would be best for the movie.

As if disappointed that I wasn't engaging in what could have been a juicy fight, he yelled, "You are acting very mature! Why are you acting so mature?"

"Well, Paul, one of us has to be," I replied, and strolled out of the makeup trailer.

But once I was back in my own trailer, I started panicking again: *Shit, how do I deal with this gracefully? I'll be "emotionally detached" if I can just figure out what to say, and how to say it without him having a massive hissy fit.*

Then there was a knock at my door. It was Paul. *Fuck.* I invited him in and said in my most soothing, adultlike voice, "Let's sit down and talk about this. I, too, want this film to be as good as it can possibly be."

Before I knew it, something took over and I was simply a passenger along for the ride.

When I was at NYU, my boyfriend at the time and I decided that we wanted to do a production of *Dutchman* by playwright LeRoi Jones (who later changed his name to Amiri Baraka). The 1964 Obie Award–winning play explored racial animosity in America in that era, as well as some of the political and psychological conflicts that Black men had to face.

I played Lula, a crazy white chick who eventually

murders Clay, a young Black man, on a subway car. I was very "method" in those days. I was still learning how to act and I was in a phase where I thought I had to stay in character at all times. I didn't really grasp how dangerous it was to be riding the subway at three in the morning from downtown to the Upper East Side, where I was living. I carried a knife in my pocket like Lula and convinced myself everything would be okay.

Late one night, however, I found myself alone on the 6 train with seven tough-looking guys. One of them began staring at me in this really creepy way. Then another guy joined in.

"Hey, baby, what're you doing out so late?"

It felt like this situation could turn against me in a heartbeat. I wasn't sure how to get out of it, so without really thinking, I started acting like an insane motherfucker. I had once seen a batshit lady slapping imaginary paste on her head while mumbling to herself, and everyone around her had instinctively moved to the other side of the street.

So, when in doubt, you have to out-crazy the crazy. I started putting imaginary paste in my hair and babbling weird shit. I might have been going over my lines, I have no idea—all I know is that it worked. The guys in that subway car recognized that I was a loon, and suddenly the tables had turned—they were scared of *me*! I heard one of them whisper, "Shit, man, she's nuts, leave her alone."

I kept up my act, hand on the knife in my pocket just in case, until I got off the train, then I hightailed it home.

* * *

When Paul sat down on the couch in my trailer, I became giddy, bursting with enthusiasm: "I have a great idea, I'm so excited! I've figured out a really great way we can do this!"

Paul seemed intrigued.

"Okay. So, I totally understand what you want to do with this shot, but truth be told—we've seen it. As you already pointed out, we've seen Sharon's vagina, and we will see Elizabeth's vagina. So I was thinking, well, just imagine this: It's dark. We don't know where we are. It's murky. Then pink. Then kind of fuzzy. Next thing you know, we're in Cristal's dressing room . . . But wait! How did we get here? We then realize we've been inside of me! We have been *inside* Cristal's vagina!! Instead of just showing my pussy like Sharon and Elizabeth, let's do the shot from *inside* my vagina! Not just the labia. Big deal, that's been done. We can even use a microscopic probe lens! No one has ever seen that before. It's brilliant—we are INSIDE MY VAGINA!!!"

Nodding his head with a bit of a smile, Paul said, "I don't know if we could get away with that."

"Oh, c'mon," I pressed, "if we're going to do it, let's REALLY do it!!" I was practically yelling at this point.

We had arrived at the moment of truth: would he call my bluff?

To my utter relief, Paul slowly backed out of my trailer, looking at me like I was bonkers, and said, "No, it's okay, we will do the scene as written. Forget I said anything."

He never mentioned my vagina again.

* * *

Showgirls was not an easy film to make, as should be obvious by now. Paul and I fought to the very end, though he was always big enough to be honest with himself (and me) after certain days of arguing—about whether or not to utilize my ever-present coke ring, for example, or the way I wanted to play a scene, or the size of a stupid hat. He would come to me and tell me that he appreciated what I had done, sometimes even saying things like: "You were right and I was wrong."

I remember how Paul wanted to include a bloody tampon swiping the frame during one scene, and I was livid. "You cannot put that in there—seriously, it's too much," I told him. And I was absolutely appalled by the brutal rape scene late in the film. *Why is this scene even here?!* I wondered. I had told my family that the movie was very funny for the most part, but our row was the only one laughing during the premiere. *Not a good sign,* I thought. Yet upon seeing the film again in 2024, the first time in years, it struck me that the rape scene, where the perpetrator gets away scot-free, is the epitome of how ugly America can be, how people in power can get away with anything as long as they continue to turn a profit.

So hats off to you, Paul: you were right and I was wrong. That scene absolutely belongs. I used to explain *Showgirls* as a modern-day version of *All About Eve* set in Vegas, and now I can better appreciate its social commentary on this country. For the first time, I really saw the movie as an indictment of the American dream. The *dark* side of that dream, with our excess, greed, and obsession with fame, fortune, and power.

Who's the Lezzie Now?

When I was cast as Corky in *Bound*, there were many angles I needed to understand in order to inhabit this street-smart chick who had just been let out of prison. She was tough, yet very vulnerable, and untrusting when it came to intimate relationships. At the start of the film, we find her working as a plumber, before it's revealed that she was involved in a robbery and had served time in the slammer.

In preparation, I had a plumber show me a thing or two; I got five more piercings in my ears so that my lock-picking tools were readily available; and I cut off my nails and hair in order to butch myself up.

I had just finished *Showgirls* a few weeks earlier and needed to change my physicality from lean, femme, and diva to introverted, suspicious, and buff. I studied the animalism of Marlon Brando in *A Streetcar Named Desire*, the quietness of Montgomery Clift in *A Place in the Sun*, and, of course, the intensity of my favorite bad boy, Robert Mitchum, in *The Night of the Hunter*. They all had certain qualities that resonated with Corky. But I still needed something else.

I wanted to come across as standoffish yet alert.

Someone who kept everyone at arm's length, revealing nothing, constantly reading the room, ready to pounce at any given moment. I wanted to project the ultimate rebel—the kind girls fall in love with. The silent, brooding type. I also wanted the precise, still, and elegant calmness of Sugar Ray Robinson. So when a friend mentioned a good private boxing gym on La Brea run by a pro named Phil Paolina, I immediately started training with him.

I had boxed a bit years before, at Gleason's Gym in Brooklyn. At the time, Naked Angels had been staging our first benefit, which featured a boxing match set in 1948, Finklestein vs. Vincente, with Fisher Stevens playing Finklestein, and Charle Landry playing Vincente. We even got the real Eddie Fisher, renowned actor and recording artist of the 1950s, to sing the national anthem. Nancy Travis and I played the boxers' girlfriends, who ended up getting into a choreographed catfight in the middle of the ring after the fifth round (if memory serves). The other Naked Angels were all dressed up and playing different characters. It was really fun and the first of many crazy benefits we performed as a company in order to stay afloat.

Boxing is one of the toughest workouts I've ever done, and I really got into the speed bag. I like the metaphor of always keeping your fists up—being prepared for anything. But I wasn't capturing the stillness I was after. When jabbed, I'd lose my cool and flail out a few punches—no doubt an old reaction caused by Dann, who liked to pin me down and torture me with the disgusting loogie-in-your-face game (a big-brother classic).

One afternoon, I showed up on La Brea to train with Phil, only to have him tell me that I needed to get into the ring and spar with a partner. He said it would help me achieve the zen I was after. He also said he had the perfect partner for me, and called a guy over.

"Bob, Gina—Gina, Bob."
"Hey, Gina."
"Hey . . . Um, Phil, can I talk to you for a second?"
We stepped off to the side.
"Dude," I said, "that's Bob Dylan. I can't hit Bob Dylan."
"You need to get in the ring with someone. You guys are a great match. Trust me."
As we were gearing up, I told Bob that I'd be starting a new shoot in a week: "Just please don't hit me in the face. My nose has already been broken. Twice."
"What are you shooting?"
"I'm doing a movie."
"But you're a musician," Bob said.
"Uhhh, no. I do play Jew's harp and sing a bit, but I'm basically an actress."
"I've always wanted to play the Jew's harp."
"I can teach you, if you like." *Oh my god, Gina, shut up! What the fuck?* "Oh yeah, I'll teach you how to play the Jew's harp, Bob Dylan." *OMG, you sound like an idiot.* This whole thing was surreal.

Then the bell rang.

We circled each other until he very gently jabbed at my face.

I snapped.

Without thinking, I threw a right hook as hard as I could at Bob's jaw—and he went down.

I froze. I hadn't hit someone like that since the Stewart Buttsky incident. A little voice in my head said, *You just broke Bob Dylan's jaw. You will go down in history as the villain who broke this legend's jaw.*

Practically in tears, I dropped down to the floor next to him. "I'm sorry! I'm so sorry!" I was mortified.

Bob started laughing and said, "I need a good woman to kick my ass every now and then."

We became sparring partners and good friends after that. I love him.

Now that I'd butched myself up with boxing, I felt more physically prepared for my new role. I was going in every day and pummeling those bags. My hands were all cut up, but I was getting ripped the way I needed to get ripped. Still, there was so much more I had to explore.

I had never cruised a gay bar. I'd never even picked up a girl or a guy before. No one ever believes that, but it's true. I hardly ever make the first move. Not out of ego, more out of shyness. Just because I have arched eyebrows doesn't mean I'm a femme fatale. And there was a whole sapphic lingo that I needed to tap into and understand.

The Wachowskis hooked me up with Susie Bright,

a feminist sexpert and master of lesbian erotica. She became the adviser for the sex scenes between me and Jennifer Tilly, who played Violet, my love interest in the film. Susie invited me to San Francisco so that she could take me around to all her favorite hot spots. Great. I could also get my look together—hair, tattoos, eyebrows. Whatever felt inspiring. So I flew up to the Bay Area for a night.

As soon as I landed, Susie apologized and told me she had some family event she'd forgotten about, so she'd be sending me off by myself. "You'll be fine. It's easier to get into some trouble on your own," she said with a wink, before giving me the names of three clubs to check out.

At the time, I was hardly a recognizable face—especially with my short hair. I had been mostly a character actor, except for *Cocktail* and *Red Heat*. Everything would change with *Showgirls,* but that hadn't come out yet.

I was going out to get some inspiration for Corky and perhaps get lucky at some bar. At the first spot, I sat down and ordered a drink. Immediately, these two girls came over to me. One of them was a long-haired beauty, a dead ringer for a Botticelli Venus. The other was a short, cute girl who looked just like Tom Cruise. They asked if they could join me and I said sure. They wanted to know when I had come out. Right away, I just felt like a jerk lying to them. I couldn't keep up the facade, so I told them the truth—that I was doing research for a movie. My two new friends laughed and one of them said, "We're your girls! We'll take you around."

The first club they took me to had a long stairway that led into a dark, cavernous space. When my eyes adjusted, I noticed a woman on all fours being fisted. There were girls making out all over the place, dressed in leather, studs, and vinyl. This club was hardcore. We had some drinks and got to know each other a little more. I thought I'd be bold and, if I got drunk enough, hit on Botticelli. She was absolutely beautiful. After a bit, they suggested we move on to another club.

The next place had more of a dance vibe. Another round of drinks. We were slowly getting tanked, and a show had begun. Three very large women in overalls, mining hats, and dark glasses got onto the stage and formed a line, facing the audience, arms akimbo. A woman from the audience walked boldly onto the stage, into the spotlight, and uncermoniously pulled down her pants and underwear. The toughest-looking miner then whipped out a straight razor and began shaving off the half-naked woman's pubic hair. Everyone in the audience was hooting and hollering and more people started lining up. I guess it was Balding Your Bush Night.

After the first woman was completely shaved, another one appeared on the stage. It should've been scary, but it actually seemed joyous and comical and everyone was having a great time. Caught up in the action, Botticelli handed me her drink and ran over to the stage. Tom Cruise and I were laughing like crazy. I guess we were pretty wasted at this point. Music was blaring and we were soon dancing wildly. So wildly, in fact, that we knocked into each other and we both fell over. Through our hysteria, I noticed a cut above her left eyebrow; our heads had collided, and there was blood trickling down her face.

"Oh my god!" I shrieked, and reached my hand out to wipe the blood off her brow.

Just then Botticelli reappeared, shoving my arm away, and yelled, "GO WASH YOUR HANDS!"

I reached toward Tom Cruise's brow once again, and said, "But look, she's bleeding."

"GO WASH YOUR HANDS RIGHT NOW! SHE WAS DIAGNOSED WITH HIV YESTERDAY! GO WASH YOUR HANDS!"

That sobered me up pretty quick. I rose to my feet in a haze and headed to the bathroom. As I scrubbed my hands, I recalled this intense dream I'd had just a few days before that I couldn't quite get my head around. I was in some sort of plutonium-processing plant—kind of like in the movie *Silkwood*. I was wearing a hazmat suit and navigating my way through a field of water balloons filled with urine, trying not to step on any of them. But I tripped and fell, and my right hand—which had cuts all over it from my boxing—landed on one of the balloons. When I stood back up, alarm bells started ringing. I looked down at my wounded hand and wondered if I had gotten infected.

Back in the club, I stared at the little cuts on my hands and felt scared and totally weirded out. What was I thinking?

The three of us left the bar and had a somber bowl

of soup at a nearby restaurant as they explained the situation to me. I went back to my hotel, and left for LA the next morning.

It had been an intense and informative night. Not only had I gained a small understanding of a whole new world, I had also figured out my look and now had insight into how I wanted to play Corky.

I was relieved to hear a few weeks later that my party girls were doing alright.

And now it was time to start filming.

I do love prep, but still, one must be careful. I had assumed that I was completely safe, immune to any dangers of the world, just because I was in a room full of women. Naive thinking on my part. Infectious diseases can descend on anyone.

Prepare, but be aware.

Driven

My agents told me I needed to do a commercial movie. They wanted to make me a viable star so they could make more money and we could land A-list projects. I had a tendency to take on dark, strange, independent features. They handed me the script for a film called *Driven* that Sylvester Stallone was going to star in and direct. It didn't feel like my cup of tea, but they urged me to meet with Stallone anyway.

Sly, as his friends call him, was a very nice guy. He was a real Renaissance man—into painting, writing, directing, and much more sensitive than I would have imagined. And let's face it, you've got to respect the guy for not only writing the screenplay for *Rocky* but holding out when people wanted to make it without him. That decision shaped his entire career.

After having lunch with Sly, I was in. I didn't totally relate to the story, but I was excited to work with him. It was about Formula One race car drivers. I would play the ex-wife to Stallone's character, a retired driver training all these young bucks.

The project took place over many months in Montreal and Toronto. Some of the actors were working with professional race car drivers, and since I wasn't in every scene, I had a lot of downtime. It was pretty cool to be around all these drivers and their cars. So when the boys were getting lessons, I thought to myself, *That'd be a great thing to learn how to do.*

I kept asking Sly if it was okay for me to learn how to drive one of the cars.

He kept saying, "Well, listen, if they have time . . ."

I felt like a broken record—like Tracy's little sister, begging to be included. When else would I get this opportunity?

In the end, no one taught me how to drive a race car. Of course, that's totally fair—it costs a lot of money and takes a lot of time. It would have been a bonus, but it wasn't at all a necessity.

The last day of shooting, however, Sly came up to me and said, "There's press out here today. I think it'd be good if you could put on a driving uniform and helmet and take a few pictures in front of one of the cars. Great publicity."

In my mind, I was like, *Oh, so I can dress up for it, but I can't actually do it.* It felt a little disingenuous.

Before I realized what was coming out of my mouth, I said I would do the photos as long as I could drive the car as well.

"Did you train with the drivers?"

"Yes," I lied, without batting an eyelash.

"Okay, sure, that'll be fine. Suit up, drive, and take some pictures."

I didn't know the first thing about driving these cars. As I was walking to the wardrobe department to get dressed, I saw one of the professional drivers, so I grabbed him and said, "Pretend I'm a computer and download step by step how you drive a race car. Don't skip any steps—I get in the car, put on the seat belt, etcetera."

The driver complied, then I went on my way, repeating like a mantra in my head, *Step one . . . Step two . . . Step three . . .*

When I got to the racetrack, there were hundreds of people. There were also way too many cameras, and the young women from production were whooping my name in sisterly solidarity.

Step one . . . Step two . . . Step three . . . Step four . . .

After I slid into the car, Sly leaned through the window and said, "The first time I drove this, I stalled. Kip stalled, Christian too. So don't worry . . ."

Step five . . . Step six . . . "There's no way I'm gonna stall."

When Sly walked away, I started the car and immediately took off like a rocket. Holy shit, it was scary! I have no idea how fast I was going, but being that close to the asphalt, with the seat so low and reclined, basically lying down, it felt pretty fucking fast. I had to remind myself to breathe without moving my arms at all or else the car would veer wildly off the track. Once I got the hang of it, I drove farther than I was supposed to, and thought I had better turn around and go back. Whoopsie—I clearly needed a bit more practice with those hairpin turns, because I kind of, very slightly, clipped the rear end of the car on the roundabout where I was making my turn.

Oh well, just a three-million-dollar vehicle—all good. When I circled back, all the production women were cheering. Sly came up to the car and said, "Hey, that was pretty good!"

He never found out that was my virgin ride.

The next morning, I woke up and could barely move my arms. You have to keep your elbows really tight against your body in one of those cars or you might veer off the track. It's a *serious* workout. Like lifting three hundred pounds of moving steel for minutes at a time.

The day after that, I literally could not lift my arms *at all*.

I did that movie for all the wrong reasons, but driving that car made the whole thing worth it. An unexpected, unanticipated, glorious nugget. Although I admit it was insanely reckless to get behind the wheel of a vehicle that I didn't know how to drive. So, to all my young readers, I would like to say to you, as the late, great William Friedkin said to me when he signed my Blu-ray copy of *The Exorcist*: *Don't try this at home.*

Rock and Roll Saved My Life

One night, I went to a musical with my friend Joe Mantello—a first-class actor, Tony Award–winning director, and fellow Naked Angel. Afterward, we had a few drinks and I started telling him about an apartment I had just bought. My first. He happened to know the previous owner, an incredible singer of musical theater.

"I used to do musicals," I said. "Did you know I was a real song-and-dance girl? Maybe this is a sign."

"Maybe," Joe replied.

More drinks.

"I think I'm supposed to do a musical again!" I enthused.

We laughed.

When I stumbled into my apartment hours later, I noticed the message light was beeping on my phone.

"Hello, Gina, this is Sam Mendes. We met at *Saturday Night Live* a few months back. Sorry to be calling you at home, but I was wondering if you'd be interested in coming into *Cabaret*, the one running on Broadway that I've directed. I think you'd be brilliant as Sally Bowles. Please give me a call back."

That Joe Mantello sure is funny, I thought. *He must have run home to make that call.*

I passed out.

The next morning, I listened to the message again. And again. And one more time. *Holy shit—that isn't Joe! I think it's actually Sam Mendes*—the gifted director of one of the best Broadway shows I'd ever seen. And Sally Bowles is one of those characters who each actor can really make her own. I had never been in a Broadway show, much less replaced someone, but I couldn't wait to start figuring out this iconic character. And yes, to sing John Kander and Fred Ebb's incredible songs.

Had the musical gods heard my request? Was this super-fantastic manifesting or just plain coincidence?

This kind of thing had only happened to me once before—when I felt like I was in some strange vortex on top of a cliff overlooking the rough sea in Cape Town, South Africa. I had loudly proclaimed, fist to sky, that I would swim with a great white shark and read *One Thousand and One Nights*. These random ideas emerged from a conversation I was having with a local man who had talked me into climbing straight up Lion's Head Mountain at daybreak. He had flattered me by saying, "You climb like a baboon," and taken me to this magical hiking spot only a few people knew about. I'd been up all night doing mushrooms and thought this was a great idea.

Afterward, I had hopped on my return flight back to LA, and just as I opened the door to my apartment, the phone rang. It was Liz, my voice-over agent.

"Darling, you just got two job offers," she squealed. This was surprising since she had not yet succeeded in booking anything for me. "The first one is they want you to narrate *One Thousand and One Nights* for the Reading Channel."

"Whoa, that's bonkers! What's the second?"

"They want you to do a documentary on the great white shark."

Okay, this was cuckoo bananas. More on this in a minute.

I immediately called Sam Mendes back and gleefully accepted his offer. Then I rang Joe to tell him the fantastic—albeit weird—news.

"No way!"

"Can you believe it?"

"That's crazy!"

Cabaret turned out to be one of the best jobs in my career up to that point.

At that same time, Alex Steyermark was getting ready to direct an indie movie called *Prey for Rock & Roll*, based on the true story of a female punk-rock musician whose career never quite blossomed. Alex didn't know I could sing, though he still thought I might be perfect for the lead role. After seeing *Cabaret*, he immediately offered it to me. He asked if I could also play the guitar and I told him I'd been playing since I was eleven. I'd set the instrument aside in my pursuit of becoming a serious actress, but as I had told Joe, I was a song-and-dance girl at heart. My first gigs had all been musicals: *Bye Bye Birdie, The Music Man, Hello, Dolly!, Faces on the Wall*. I was even the dancing legs in the film *Beatlemania*. *Cabaret* had reawakened my love of singing.

Alex sent me the script for *Prey for Rock & Roll* and I fucking loved it. It was a story that dealt with what it meant to hit a certain age as an entertainer when you still haven't really "made it." Whether you're an artist, writer, actor, dancer, painter—what happens when you haven't been able to earn a living doing what you love? At what point do you give it up, and *how* do you give it up?

I told Alex I was on board.

We had to record the music for the film, and the incomparable Joan Jett was hired to be my guitar player. I asked her to coach me on playing electric guitar, since I'd only ever played an acoustic. In a very Joan Jett way, she said, "Spread your legs, place the guitar against your cunt, and pretend you're jerking off." I really appreciate specific directions. She even gave me the leather choker she often sported, which I tied around my neck and wore throughout the film.

At some point, however, all of the financing for the movie fell through. But I was totally committed at that point, and we'd already recorded the music—so Alex recruited me to take on the additional role of a producer. We had a shortfall of $1.5 million and we were supposed to start filming in three weeks.

I kicked into maniac mode, went to the Cannes Film Festival with my producer hat on, and within two days I'd gotten the money. Now let me just say:

I prefer to be in a movie where everything is taken care of and I can just act. But sometimes, if you really want to do something, you just have to do it yourself. And sometimes sacrifices must be made.

Back to the great white shark documentary: one thing led to another, and the guy making the film—the guy who would actually be in the water, sans cage, with the great white—had asked me to join him . . . to *swim* with the great white shark! Just as I had proclaimed up on that mountaintop!

I *had* to do it, much to my family's dismay. My brother told me I was low on the ocean food chain and should probably rethink this. What was the worst that could happen . . . ? I die? Well, yeah. Okay. There's that. Fair. But at least I would face my fear.

Alas, there was a scheduling conflict that couldn't be remedied: the week that I would have been swimming with (and possibly being eaten by) the great white shark coincided exactly with the recording of the music for Alex Steyermark's film, which had to be completed before we could start shooting. Being a professional, it was an easy decision. You could say that rock and roll saved my life.

The making of *Prey for Rock & Roll* was an incredible experience. We got invited to the Sundance Film Festival and I was asked by the financiers and other producers to play an actual rock gig to help promote the film. I said, "I don't have a band." They said, "Figure it out."

I had no idea how to do this.

Fortunately, two hours later while out on a donut run, I happened to bump into my new friend Matt Sorum—the drummer of Guns N' Roses. I asked if he had any advice about how I could quickly put a band together to play this gig. Matt said, "*I'll* be your drummer. And how about I ask Slash and Duff to come on, too?" Slash, of course, is Guns N' Roses's iconic guitarist; and Duff McKagan is their incredible bass player. Within five minutes of my conversation with Matt, both of them were in.

I called the other producers on the film and shared the news: "I've got Guns N' Roses to be my band. You don't need to pay them, but you need to pay their travel expenses."

This is why I admire musicians so much: they really just want to *play*! If I was dealing with an actor, I would've ended up on the phone for weeks, with all sorts of agents, managers, and lawyers, trying to figure out paperwork and schedules. Later on, when I was making an actual record featuring music from the film, musicians I know were upset when I *didn't* ask them to participate. I ended up recording with some truly amazing players—not just Matt and Slash, but also Christian McBride, Ivan Neville, Linda Perry, Leroy Powell, Chris Powell, and others.

The gig went so well that one of the film producers said, "You should go on tour to promote the film as it's premiering around the country." Fun idea, yet they offered absolutely no money.

I asked, "How am I supposed to *tour*? Throw my guitar in a little red wagon? I need an actual band, not just friends doing me a favor."

In came Seth Jarrett, soon to be one of my producers. "Why don't we do a reality show? I think I can get money from IFC if we do a tour and you film it."

At the time, reality shows were just getting their legs, and I was secretly kind of against them. I told Seth I'd only do it if it could be a six-part program—more of a docuseries than a reality show. If only I could consult with D.A. Pennebaker, who had made *Don't Look Back,* a stellar documentary about Bob Dylan.

Well, that night I had to go to some benefit, and guess who I happened to be seated next to? D.A. Pennebaker himself. Sometimes things happen because they're *supposed* to happen. This whole trajectory just kept falling into place. I picked Pennebaker's brain and he graciously advised: "Make it like a whole movie and cut it up into six parts."

Next, I had to find a band. I went downtown to my favorite breakfast joint, Bubby's, and used it as my office. I ended up interviewing many a band, and ultimately decided to go with three members of a super-cool indie-rock band based in New York called Girls Against Boys. The lineup was Scott McCloud on guitar, Alexis Fleisig on drums, and Johnny Temple on bass. I cannot tell you how much fun I had touring with these guys.

* * *

The tour was three weeks long. Before we hit the road, Cheri Lovedog—whose story *Prey for Rock & Roll* is based on—reached out and told me that in her experience, the songs I played in the movie didn't go over well live. (The whole point is that she never quite made it as a musician. Duh.) So, I had to figure out more music to add to our set. I started writing songs like a crazy person, and I was lucky enough that some great musicians helped me, one of them being the fantastic Linda Perry.

I really loved doing these gigs. We played a bunch of cool little clubs all across America. In the mornings, I'd have to get up and promote the film as an actress. But by night we'd party like, well, you know, rock stars. On a budget. Unfortunately, along the way it became clear that the movie wasn't being released where it was supposed to be released; the "distributors" weren't really doing their job. They sort of tanked the project—no one knew where the movie would be playing, not even me. This led to very dramatic moments during the tour. The good news was that the worse the situations became, the better it was for the docuseries, which we called *Rocked with Gina Gershon*.

Sometimes jobs lead you to paths you weren't initially thinking of going down. And although people couldn't figure out where to see the film, this experience was pushing me back to my first love: music. While traveling, I caught the bug and started writing more music. By the end of the tour, I had a whole album in my head. Our set featured maybe three songs from the movie, and the band and I were having a great time playing whatever else we were playing. This led to other gigs where people started actually paying us.

The point of all this is that sometimes you just have to stay in the flow, because you never know where it's going to take you. Doing *Cabaret* on Broadway led me to filming *Prey for Rock & Roll*, which led me to playing live and touring, which led me to making a record, which led me to performing it as a one-woman show downtown at the Box, which led to David Kuhn, an incredible book agent and friend, getting me a deal to write *In Search of Cleo: How I Found My Pussy and Lost My Mind*, which eventually led me to creating another show, *Wild Women Don't Get the Blues*, which I performed at the legendary Café Carlyle.

None of it really makes sense. I was supposed to be mapping out my acting career. Instead, I followed the fun. The best parts of my career and life have happened when I've been guided by the energy to take me on a journey I never planned.

Prey for Rock & Roll came out for maybe two weeks, got great reviews, and then just disappeared. Twenty years later, when I participated in a Comic-Con autograph signing during the 2023 SAG-AFTRA strike, I was surprised by how many people had the original DVD for *Prey for Rock & Roll*. Others kept coming up to me and asking, "Why can't we find that movie anywhere?" I remember calling Alex and telling him, "People really wanna see this film."

One thing led to the other, and next thing I knew, Kino Lorber rereleased it and now it can finally be found on most platforms for your viewing pleasure. I'm very proud of this film.

And just one more fun fact: my bass player who I went on tour with for *Prey for Rock & Roll*, Johnny Temple, happens to be the publisher and editor of this book you're reading. While we were out partying after a gig, he was diligently going through piles of manuscripts, and when I asked him one night what he was doing, he humbly replied, "I've started a publishing house." And here we are today. Nice job, Johnny.

Afterword
President of the Girls League

I like to know the truth. For better or worse. Even if it hurts. I can appreciate someone trying to spare my feelings from unpleasant information, but the frequency of a lie vibrates in my body and feels much more unsettling and disturbing than any hard truth. Sometimes (most of the time?) things don't work out, whether it's in business or personal relationships. But I'd rather be disappointed than disillusioned any day of the week.

Like Socrates once said, "Know thyself." As an actor, I've found this to be essential. To truly embody a character and access deep, honest emotion, you have to be willing to examine your own inner world. That's what I love about artists, whether actors, writers, poets, musicians, or painters: they are seekers of truth. They observe, explore, and express inner and outer worlds with courage, using their medium as a conduit.

I loved studying with Sandra Seacat and now her daughter Greta, because their work dives well beneath the surface. It helps uncover hidden truths, buried emotions, and psychic wounds that often dictate how we move through life. Certain therapies have been profoundly helpful too. Knowing yourself is the foundation for living in truth: grounded, resilient, and free from the manipulation of others. The stories I've shared—about pressure, bullies, and the artistic nooses I've had to wriggle free from—are snapshots of my journey: how I navigated discomfort and what I've learned from it. We have a responsibility to ourselves to stay aware, to choose wisely, and to trust our feelings. And just to be clear—I'm not talking about navigating truly dangerous people: psychopaths, abusers, or predators. Those, of course, we avoid at all costs. I've never met a snake, wolf, or wildcat I couldn't get along with—but that doesn't mean I'd walk alone through a jungle at midnight.

I love a good massage. And by that, I mean a deep-tissue, pain-releasing, get-that-knot-out-NOW kind of massage. Light, relaxing ones? They drive me nuts. I want to feel the pressure where it hurts and break through. Same with therapy. I'm not one for endless talk. I like to plunge into the source, dig out the root, and move forward. I was lucky to find Dr. Mary Lou Rane, a practitioner of NET (Neuro Emotional Technique)—part therapist, part psychic detective. NET works by identifying how trauma is stored in the body. Through muscle testing, tapping, kinesiology, and memory work, we traced my old emotional imprints and belief systems, and cleared them. That work changed my life.

As I mentioned at the beginning of this book, I discovered that my mother didn't know she was pregnant with me until six months in. That truth emerged during a session with Mary Lou, when I was working through my discomfort with asking for help. I'd always been hyper-independent. When she traced the emotion back to the womb and inquired what was going on then, I said, "How am I supposed to know what happened then? I was in the womb!"

"Ask your mother," she replied. And there it was—the missing piece.

When I first began dreamwork and deeper therapy, I found myself feeling distant and angry toward my mother—emotions I hadn't fully processed. I thought my wounds stemmed from losing my father at nineteen. But as we dug further, a new moment surfaced. I remembered being questioned by police about a sexual predator (see "Danger in the Trees") and feeling exposed, unsupported.

With Mary Lou's encouragement, I brought it up with my mom. Her response was defensive at first, but I couldn't hold back. I raged out my feelings to her about the whole matter. She asked, "Do you think I was a good mother?" and without hesitation, I said no. She cried. She had done her best, she told me apologetically. And though I felt terrible, a long-standing emotional wall between us crumbled. From that day on, our conversations had a new honesty.

In time, I learned more about her own upbringing—especially about her mother, a narcissistic and emotionally fragile woman. About how my mom felt she needed to be perfect all the time so that she wouldn't upset her. Knowing that context gave me a greater understanding into who my mother was. Years later, she asked again, "Do you think I was a good mother?" This time, I reconsidered and responded, "I think you did the best you could." She accepted that.

Right before the COVID pandemic, she was diagnosed with cancer. True to form, she fought it like a champ, got radiation, and moved through it with grace, even creating a chic new look for herself. When she was losing her hair, as one sometimes does with treatment, I was surprised when my vain mother shaved off her remaining tufts and announced that she had a perfectly round head. It was uncanny. She was one of the few white women who could actually pull off a bald head. But as her hair grew back, now silver and black, she cut it into a smart little 'do, changed her wardrobe palette, and looked more stylish than ever.

By then she had been living in a lovely assisted-living community. It felt like summer camp for seniors. I joked about her finding a boyfriend there, though it was a competitive scene—one woman even staked her claim on the only eligible man by making out with him in front of my mom. My sister and I dubbed some of the other residents "the casserole ladies," the ones who appeared with food and flirtation the minute someone's wife died. Truth is, we all want someone to share the news with and complain to. I suggested we sign her up on a senior dating site, and she said, "Honey, at my age all they want is the nurse or the purse." (*The Nurse or the Purse*: potentially a winning idea for a senior reality show.)

* * *

I was in Los Angeles when the lockdown hit. I was supposed to be making what would have been the funniest movie ever with Trey Parker and Matt Stone, the brilliant *South Park* team, but due to the pandemic, filming was canceled. (Another dream shattered.)

This, however, allowed me to spend real time with my mom. I brought her her favorite sushi dishes, and indulged her newfound love of weed gummies. I made her tell me stories from her life: her struggles and triumphs. I learned how hard she had to fight to get her name on a credit card even though she ran her own design business, Emm Gee Interiors. How she deflected inappropriate comments as a young model. And how she had left a wealthy but boring fiancé for my broke but handsome, fun, and charming father, because they fell in love with each other at station 26 at the beach club in Santa Monica.

As my mom grew weaker, we talked about death. I found it so interesting that we shared the same beliefs about death, reincarnation, and karma. We had never really talked about these concepts before, and it was reassuring to discover that we saw them in such a similar light. She asked me to help her transition when the time came. To give her the "shot," like I had my beloved cat Cleo. She knew it wasn't legally possible in California, but made me promise I'd support her choice and do what I could.

One day in a session with Mary Lou, while I was speaking about how uncomfortable I felt taking bows and celebrating my own wins, she said: "Ask your mother about that dynamic." And so I did. My mom shared a memory she'd never spoken aloud. In high school, she had run for president of the Girls League. She made posters, gave speeches . . . and won. She rushed home to tell her mother, who was playing mahjongg with friends. Her mother waved her off with a distracted "That's nice," and never mentioned it again.

As my mom recalled the story, she started to cry. Years of unacknowledged pride, shame, and hurt surfaced. But something shifted in her—her face softened, and for a moment I saw the young girl she had been, ambitious, dismissed, and unseen. Right then I felt an enormous surge of love for her. For her vulnerability, courage, and strength. As if this confession had released her from invisible constraints.

Suddenly, she felt free. And her growth became *my* growth, her shadow dissolving into the ether, taking part of my shadow along with it. It was at this moment that I finally told her, without any hesitation or prompting, that she had been, and was, a really good mother.

A few months later, while I was in West Virginia preparing to direct my first film, my sister called: "Come home. She's not doing well." I'd gotten calls like this before, and my mom had always rallied—with milkshake and meatball cravings, no less. But this time was clearly different. I flew to LA that same day.

When I entered my mom's room, she looked up at me, and I immediately knew. I said, "You're ready," and she nodded. But in true Mickey fashion, she insisted we do her hair, draw her brows, and build her lips. "Hurry, hurry," she said, as though late for a party. I wouldn't have been surprised.

When my sister and I were cleaning out her drawers, figuring out what to do with all her stuff that she'd collected throughout her life, I discovered, unceremoniously shoved in the back of an otherwise organized drawer, a small wooden hammer—a judge's mallet.

"What's that?" Tracy asked.

On closer examination, there was a tarnished brass plague wrapped around the mallet that said, *Mickey Koppel, President of the Girls League, 1949.*

We all walk our own path. I've shared a few of my stories—glimpses of how I've come to know myself, how I've made sense of life and its shadows. This is not meant to be a guidebook, just a reflection on my own journey. One of the only pieces of advice I *would* offer—whether or not you're an artist—is to learn about your parents. And not just who they were to *you*, but who they were to their own parents. Understanding their stories helps us reclaim our own. One of my favorite books is *Owning Your Own Shadow: Understanding the Dark Side of the Psyche* by Jungian psychologist Robert A. Johnson. Sometimes we carry wounds that aren't even ours. Releasing them helps us stand in our truth—free, sovereign, whole.

I've been blessed to be surrounded by fierce, brilliant, creative women throughout my life. My family, friends, and teachers. I will forever be grateful for their shared wisdom. They have inspired and guided me through my work and love life, helping me walk through the world with dignity and confidence.

*I dedicate this book to my father,
Stanley Gershon,
for making me strong,
and to my mother,
Mignonette Von Koppel,
aka Mickey Gershon,
president of the Girls League, 1949,
the first AlphaPussy I ever knew.*

Acknowledgments

I'd like to thank the following people for their support of me and this book:

David Kuhn, for always lovingly nudging a story out of me.

Laurie Anderson, a constant source of inspiration, encouragement, and that "can do" attitude.

Asti Hustvedt, for always listening and giving so generously of her time and talent.

My gang—Rosie Tang, Ev Williams, and Daniel Jones—for their enthusiastic support, wherever we may find ourselves.

My sister Tracy, for being such a badass and always being there for me.

Tanta and Joanna, for being my cheerleaders.

James Frey, for his constant support and encouragement.

Emmett O'Malley, for his enthusiasm, support, and technical skills.

Dustin Yellin, for his artistic eye.

Damian Loeb, for his artistic patience.

Mary Lou Rane, who has helped me understand so much about myself.

And to you, Johnny Temple, for having the drive and discipline to read all those manuscripts in the bus, and for always staying true to the beat.